AF365604

HOW TO BECOME A NONFICTION AUTHOR

Tips to Writing & Self Publishing a Book Without Losing Your F*cking Mind

MALENE BENDTSEN

Publishing Rebel disclaims all responsibility and liability for your use of any information found in this book or related web pages. Information provided in this book is for educational purposes only. Publishing Rebel cannot guarantee the accuracy of the information and is not responsible for any missing information.

ISBN: 978-87-974785-0-9 (audio)
ISBN: 978-87-972095-9-2 (ebook)
ISBN: 978-87-972095-7-8 (hardback)
ISBN: 978-87-972095-8-5 (paperback)
Cover & Layout: Diren Yardimli

www.publishing-rebel.com

Immediate access to writing tips and author coaching:

10

44

198

INTRO

PATH

FANDANGO

Content Clues

Nonfiction Ninja Perks

Author income

Authority

Attraction

Autonomy

Adventure

A   12

Your Brain: The Funky Edition

6 myths you don't give a sh*t about

Dying from boredom writing your book

The only 3 things that truly matter for you

B   26

The Rebel Method

The most common fuckups to avoid

The Rebel Method: 6 P's of self publishing

C   34

Plan: Scoping Voyage to Victory

Calculating bestseller ROIs

Positioning your book for success

The 3 cornerstones of your marketing plan

1   46

Produce: First Draft Dash-o-thon

How to not let your brain fuck it up for you

Writing better and faster

Unfuck writer's block

2   94

Pre-sell: Beyoncé your way to the top

Lessons from bestselling authors

How to wisely combine boring sh*t and fun sh*t

Maintaining 100% ownership

3   126

Polish: Perfecting your masterpiece

Taking your manuscript to the highest level

Book cover fuckups and what to do instead

Bestselling book formats

Pre-publication decisions

4   136

Publish: Print, Pixel & POD Potpourri

Print distribution vs. print-on-demand

The 3 digital formats

Selling with metadata

The 99% cases where launch-day doesn't matter

5   158

Promote: Marketing Bonanza

Sprint vs. Marathon

When to advertise and when not to

Getting in front of crowds

Getting reviews

6   178

The Fandango

Funky fresh marketing ideas

Author Bio

Endnotes

198

Hi, I am Malene!

Being an expert on whatever you teach, you know a book will be the jewel in your book-empowered teaching or speaking empire. You are completely aware that the potential profits from a book go way beyond book sales. You know a book will be the single most important asset you'll ever create for your business. You also know that you can write a great book and audaciously promote it without blushing.

This condensed, visually appealing, no-fluff, non-boring, but opinionated book will help you:

- Write the right book for your business
- Get published faster and with less hassle
- Know the secrets of bestselling authors

I suspect you are a person who never runs out of ideas. If you are like most of the thought leaders I've worked with facilitating the birth of dozens of books, your biggest struggle is to stick to one idea before moving on to the next. There is a reason this particular idea of publishing a book stuck with you. The time has come for you to pursue the next level in your business adventure.

I am Malene, a writing and publishing coach, and a book editor specialising in helping solopreneurs with a teaching or public speaking business become nonfiction authors. I am here to make you fall in love with your book.

Vamos!!

Malene Bendtsen
Publishing Rebel & Knowledge Liberator

The
INTRO

Blazing Bestseller Trails

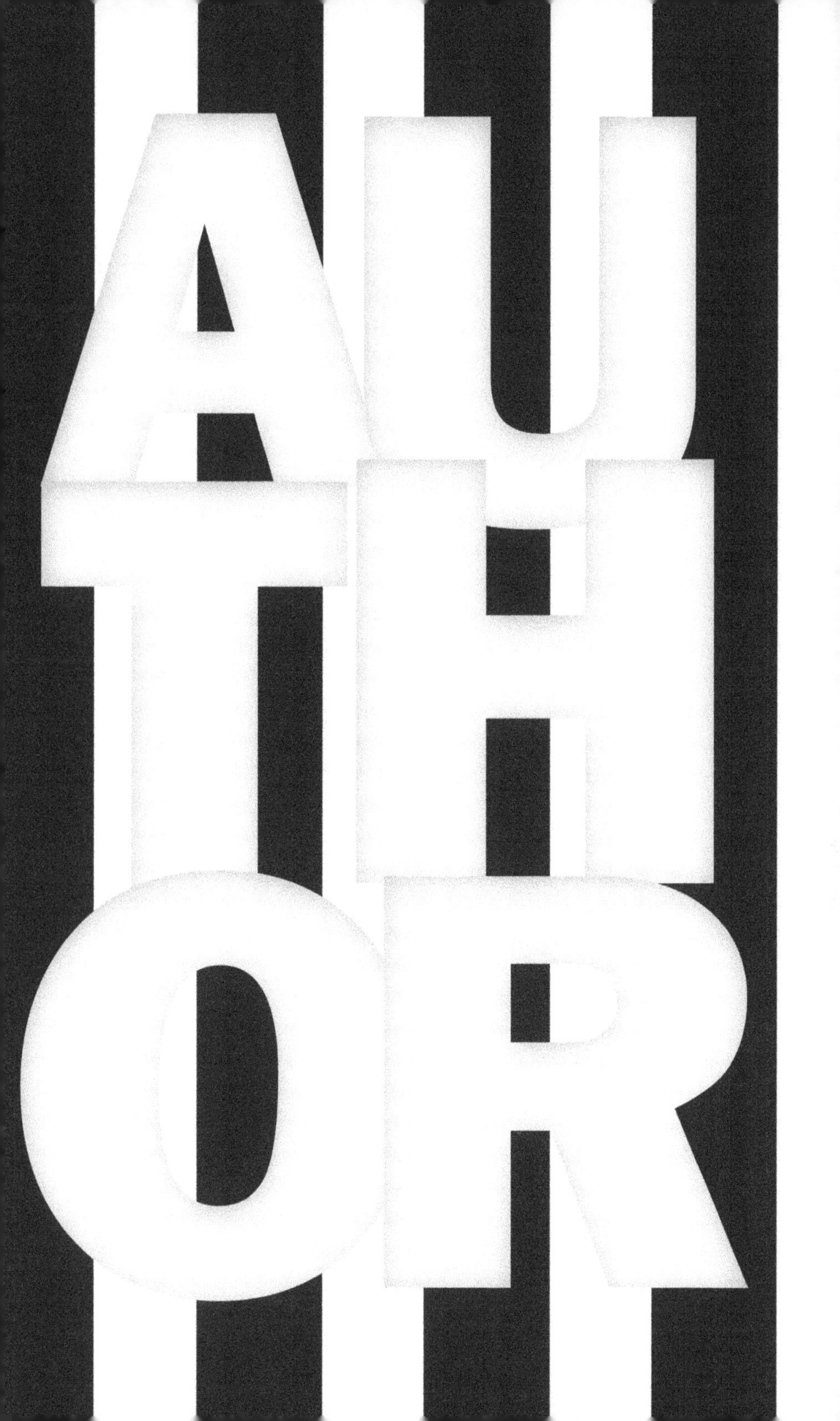

chapter A

Nonfiction Ninja Perks

What is author success? What are the benefits and advantages you can expect from becoming an author? What are the real perks of writing and publishing a nonfiction book?

Author income

A survey[1] conducted by CREATe Centre in 2022 among 60,000 UK authors revealed that, apart from vast differences in earnings between White and Asian vs Black or mixed-race people and significant gender gaps, there is also a rapid decline in author income.

In fact, UK author income in 2022 decreased by 60% since 2006 and 38% since 2018[2]. Canada was, in 2018, down 27% since 2015[3], while the US dropped 42% from 2009 to 2018[4]. Only Australia was up 3% between 2015 and 2022[5].

I know! This is depressing news, isn't it?

Luckily, general data isn't really useful when it comes to book publishing. First of all, authors are sometimes defined quite broadly. For example, fiction authors who write long book series are included. And almost all reporting in book publishing is based on books sold in retail only (not books sold directly by the author), and furthermore only includes traditionally published authors and not self-published authors. This is also the case for the aforementioned survey. But the trajectory for traditionally published books is clear; author income is rapidly declining.

As a response to the off-putting disclosures in the CREATe report, ALLi, the Alliance of Independent Authors, conducted the world's first independent global survey of more than 2,000 authors and found that self-published authors earn significantly more than writers with third-party publishers. Uplifting news!

It should be noted that the survey included self-publishing authors who spend 50% or more of their time on their publishing activities and that the majority were fiction authors. More than half were from the US, but also the UK was well represented with 21% of respondents.

* * *

Success comes in many forms. To me, success is making my own decisions. That feeling of freedom to choose what to do, who to do it with, where I wanna do it, and for how long. I designed my business from a set of lifestyle criteria that I won't allow to be compromised. I am not looking simply to create a new job for myself but to create a life of abundance, freedom, and contribution.

My ultimate goal is to create a legacy of having helped in setting knowledge free so we can all live to our full potential and work together to create a better world. Helping you reach thousands and thousands of people with your message, knowledge, and methods, allows me to indirectly

"

The tendency for traditionally *published books is clear; author income is rapidly* declining *while self-published authors* earn *significantly* more *than writers with third-party publishers.*

Self published authors

Income report 2022

Median income app. 50% higher than traditionally published authors

The average author income was over $80,000

More than 2,000 authors have surpassed $100,000 in "royalties" from Amazon KDP

How many earn how much? (approximate numbers):

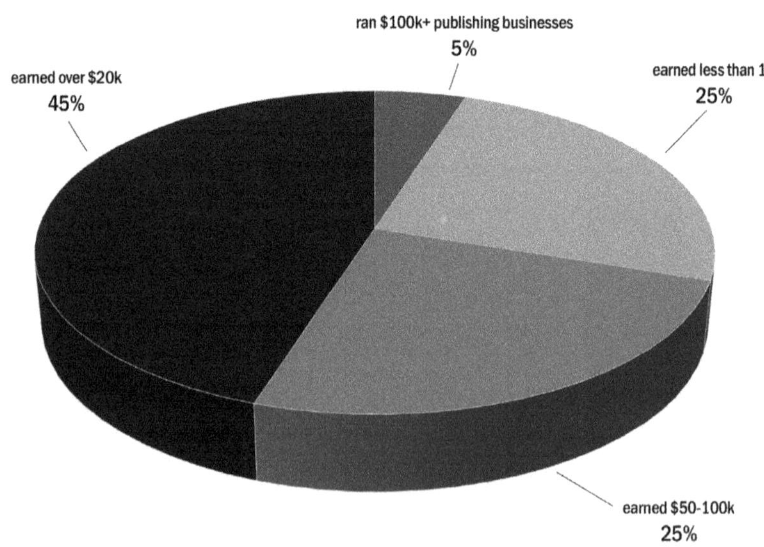

impact many more people in a variety of ways than I would ever be able to do alone. That is why this book is in your hands now.

For some, publishing a book is all about legacy and it's enough simply knowing that their ideas or story is everlasting and available to whoever it was meant for.

For others, the process of writing their book has a healing element to it. They had some kind of traumatic experience and they work through their pain as they put words on paper.

Others write because their ideas and concepts will become more crisp and they will be able to better communicate their thoughts.

Or they are driven by something more tangible like the outlook of fame, customer leads, or passive, long-term income.

There is undeniably a great potential to create significant income as a self published author. And as a nonfiction author, the book is not even your main source of income. Your plan is probably to kick ass using your book to elevate your entire business!

So while some or all of the motivations above may or may not be true for you, this book will help you achieve something I believe you desire even more than royalties from your book sale: authority, attraction, autonomy, and adventure.

Authority

It is no coincidence that almost all popular authorities have a book. Listen to the word: *Author*-ity. It's right there in the word. Becoming an author and thereby raising your authority will generate trust. As you provide your audience with an opportunity to discover your expertise and personality, you are also becoming more attractive as a speaker, podcast guest, service provider, and candidate for strategic collaborations.

Being a published author can enhance a speaker's credibility, visibility, and demand. Generally, published authors may also command higher speaking fees compared to non-published speakers due to the perceived value and expertise associated with having written and published a book. Speaking fees can vary significantly depending on the speaker's reputation, demand, speaking expertise, industry, location, length of the talk, and other relevant factors and it's challenging to provide an exact average fee for but the tendency is clear; published authors are paid higher fees.

Likewise, consultancy fees, coaching fees and other services requiring the personal time of the author can increase significantly. But perhaps the most interesting fact is that attracting and retaining customers is often a lot easier, being a recognised authority, because trust preexists through the credibility provided by the book.

"

Attracting and retaining customers is often a lot easier, being a recognised authority, *because trust pre-exists through the credibility provided by the book.*

Attraction

You don't necessarily want to be the best or the most popular. You want to be *different*, stand out and attract opportunities to work with people you admire and who light you up with their cool energy. To succeed in that, you must be known for who you truly are. And this goes far beyond being authentic (omg... are you also getting bored with that word??).

Having the best product is, without a doubt, an advantage. But your creativity, novel thoughts, inspiring personality, quirkiness, nerdiness, and weirdness, and of course the unheard-of strategies you use and methods you developed to get better results - allowing all of this to become known to the world - is a very smart business move.

The benefits don't stop there. Standing out and being ahead and being different simply makes you happy. Not for the admiration itself (yeah, ok, that's pretty awesome too). But because that's exactly how you feel about yourself; Different in the coolest way. You are not like most people and you thrive and contribute with the most value in the world when you are exploring something new.

This is one of the reasons I know you will succeed as an author; You already act as an authority in your circles. We just need to push that further out into the world so you can receive the admiration you deserve (read: sell more and sell easier), and attract people who speak your language and dance your rumba.

"*You already act as an authority in your circles.* We just need to push that *further out into the world.*

Autonomy

If something deflates you, it's a slow process in which you have to adapt and comply with other people's agendas. You get easily bored with repetitive tasks and being in the same conversation, over and over. One of the reasons you are reading this book now may very well be that you somehow managed to get stuck in boredom - in your own business. It's only natural if you are a person who craves stimuli and new experiences - enough for your brain to have new stuff to unpretzel - and to feel you are getting the most out of life.

I bet you are a huge fan of autonomy (it takes one to know one) and want to be able to move faster, aim higher, do more, and be different - when you want it and how you want it.

Publishing a nonfiction book can do that for you. It will help you with scalability in your business. To rise to the next level and have people doing the boring stuff, so you can focus on creatively kicking ass and picking where you want to speak next, or which marketing campaign might be fun to create.

The ultimate approach to achieving true autonomy in your business is to become a known authority, self publishing your book.

The ultimate approach to achieving true autonomy *in your business is to become a* known authority, *self publishing your book.*

Adventure

Exactly what an adventurous life looks like differs from one person to the next. But I am pretty sure that a part of it, for you, is closely related to autonomy and how you work; Choosing where, when and with whom you want to work, choosing your customers and business partners as you please.

I also think there is more to it than that. At least, I encourage you to be honest with yourself about what the book adventure looks like for you. Do you want it to make you an international keynote speaker travelling 200 days per year? Do you want to build a membership empire? Do you want to be able to integrate a charity-like component in your business model and spend most of your time on projects not directly related to your business, other than brand-wise? What do you want your most adventurous life to look like in 5 or 10 years?

Publishing a book is a long-term strategy and your hottest dreams should shape your authorship. Knowing how you will measure your success will not only shape your book strategy. It will quite often define the scope and set constraints for your book content too.

Either way, becoming an author will be a next-level adventure, that's for sure.

Publishing a book is a **long-term strategy** *and your* **hottest dreams** *should shape your authorship.*

chapter B

Your Brain:
The Funky Edition

Not all authors are alike so I want to give you a heads-up on what you can expect to be my viewpoint before we dive into the more practical part of this book. I wanna make sure we are on the same page (got it? ;)

6 myths you don't give a sh*t about

Let's be real. There are an insane amount of myths about book publishing. Of all the explanations and excuses I've heard over the years working with authors, the majority fall into one of six categories. I am sharing them here to debunk them and hand you a mirror to discover if any of them is the real reason you haven't taken action yet or stopped yourself from becoming an author. I know it's weird to include them in this book because I actually believe you don't give a sh*t about them. But…

I am assuming you didn't have the idea of becoming an author yesterday. If you are like most of the authors I've worked with, you have been thinking about this for a while. Something held you back. Being honest with yourself about what that is, might be the only true roadblock to your author success. You are welcome ;)

#1 - You need a great (better) book idea

The problem isn't that you don't have an idea but that you have too many ideas. That's what made you an entrepreneur in the first place. You are more than open and capable of both capturing new ideas and coming up with novel ideas. If that doesn't sit well with you, I failed at "casting" you as a reader of this book. The solution is simple: Pick one! But pick wisely because the right book can bring income for the rest of your life and even 70 years beyond. This book will teach you how to identify the perfect topic and angle of your book as well as how to maximise profits from your book.

#2 - Somebody already published a similar book

Good news! There is a market for this type of book then. Why on earth would you want to publish a book that there is no vibrant market for? You don't need a topic nobody ever wrote about before. You need to make yours different - and anything other than different coming from you just seems silly or close to impossible, doesn't it? You're okay. Just do the work.

#3 - It's expensive to self publish

You can publish a book for zero dollars. Alright, there might be areas where you would want to invest a little, like having someone remove poor grammar or creating a great design. But really, you could start skipping your daily Starbucks coffee today and you'll soon have enough to pay for a great cover design. Stop making excuses. Find a way. That's how you got this far anyway. This is no different. And you definitely don't want a traditional publisher if you want to publish faster, maintain ownership of your book, and make your own decisions. Self publishing is not the lesser choice. It's the absolute best choice for solopreneurs.

#4 - I don't have time

Please stop saying you want to write a book. Start saying you are publishing your book in June or November or whenever. Find someone to keep you accountable so you start making it a priority; A book coach, another aspiring author or your audience! Or give $1,000 to a friend and let them know they can keep it if you don't publish as planned. Choose a friend you trust to not deliver it back unless you finish your book within a certain time! If $1,000 won't do the trick for you, raise the stakes. Nobody has more time than you. Successful people make time for the things that matter the most.

#5 - I am not a writer

More good news! You don't have to be. In fact, you are already not equally good at all the work you do or have done in your business. You'll need writing done, but it doesn't have to be just you doing it, even if you are sitting with the thought, it needs to be your voice and your ideas. It will be. And if you are not a bad writer but simply a slow one, I'll teach you how to get all of that awesomeness out of your head and onto paper without writing much at all. If you are a self-diagnosed bad writer or a slow writer, the writing part is likely to be your biggest headache - until you read this book. What you need to be is a great teacher. Not a writer.

#6 - If my book is bad, it will hurt my brand

This one goes deeper and is really the cousin of imposter syndrome. Let me be clear on this: The only people whose opinion matters are your ideal customers in your business. Not your best friend who is very successful in his or her career. Not your other friend who is a great writer. Not even your spouse. If you are struggling with other people's opinions in general, listen: Other people's opinions have nothing to do with your ability to write an amazing book. It's usually the judgement and ultimate rejection from people close to them that authors with this problem fear. I want you to think about it like this: You will only succeed in attracting the people you are the best to serve if you are 100% yourself. Those who don't see the value in your work are not your people - or at least the wrong people for your business. Their opinion doesn't matter if they are not in your target audience.

Dying from boredom writing your book

Oftentimes authors, when first approaching me, tell me they "also want to write a book". My first question is always: "Do you want to write a book or have a published book?" As the confused expression on their faces evaporates, we have a talk about the writing process and how long typing out 200 pages takes (which you don't even need to do but that's for a later chapter).

Even for slow typers, there is no way it takes the number of years people claim it took to write their books. Pardon me, but if it takes years, or even one year, writing it is not the reason but rather that the author did not have a clear concept or message to share in the book. It took time because they had to learn about the subject themselves, develop key concepts, they got distracted, or they had to deal with a publisher that asked for rewrites repeatedly without properly guiding the process.

Or they used highly unproductive writing strategies that were better fit for fiction or writing as a hobby. These people inherited expectations for what becoming an author might entail that are simply not relevant for an otherwise business-savvy, badass nonfiction writer who is already teaching great stuff.

I am going to teach you how to make sure creating your manuscript can happen faster AND with a better result, using a business and teaching approach rather than outdated, dreadful writing methods designed for another time, another type of writing, and another type of author.

As the author of this book, it is my job to make sure you didn't miss that this book is written specifically for you - while also ensuring that I am attracting the right type of person.

If you feel completely out of place at this point, you'll still learn a lot in this book. But you probably won't be a good fit for my business because this is who I am. You'll hate it. I'll not be the perfect help you need. But I will still love you ;)

Putting a page like this in a book is the weirdest meta thing to do. But there is an important takeaway. When you buy a book online, did you notice the first 10% of the book is available as a preview before making a purchase? Sometimes they are called 'previews', sometimes 'look inside' or something along those lines.

This means you should do your best to sell your book on those pages. That's why it was my strategic choice to make sure you'd recognise yourself as a favourite client of mine on these first pages and that the benefits of reading it would be crystal clear. I want only badass people in my business (that's you!).

You can even add a page with a giveaway on those first pages to collect leads, even from people who choose not to buy your book for some reason.

Go ahead, you can steal that idea!

The only 3 things
that truly matter for you

If you are looking for a method to ensure writing your book will be worth the time and money you invest, you are in the right place.

It implies three things:

You need it to attract the **right customer** and you need to be able to **execute** your book project effectively to avoid too many unbillable hours spent.

And because you are you, you also need it to be absolutely **non-boring** and to be inspired with some crazy arse and surprising ideas to keep the energy going.

These three things have been my focus in this book.

chapter C

The Rebel Method

I should warn you. This book does not offer a step-by-step system invented in a one-size-fits-all approach. Instead, it educates you on the most important decisions you need to make on your journey. There is plenty of how-to information out there and even the self publishing platforms offer a lot of it, as do I in my private membership. But rarely does any of this rather fragmented information provide a full picture of the entire process or help you make the right decisions at the right time, or explain how the industry works and WHY those decisions are important to make at the right time.

You're a go-getter so you'll figure out the practical stuff. You don't need me to show you where the buttons are or how to google. You need me to teach at an overall level and educate you so you can ask the right questions and make the right decisions for your business.

The most common fuckups to avoid

Since you, in general, are a person who pays attention to what's new, you might have converted to audiobooks and podcasts and short-form entertaining videos a while ago. You'll likely listen at 1.5x speed and appreciate clickable timestamps to skip to what you need next. And I love you for it. You are a fast mover and when you want something, you simply go get it. Like a hummingbird overlooking the scene, selecting the best flowers, and then diving deep into what you want, before galaxy-hopping to the next big thing, drunk on novelty nectar. You are a person who gets sh*t done, and you don't have time for slow talk or detailed information, half of which you already knew.

I know you'll appreciate not having to discover the most common fuckups bit by bit, treasure hunting throughout the book, simply because I applied some lame "I won't give it all right away" strategy to force you to read the whole thing and fall in love with me. I am pretty sure you'll appreciate knowing where you might fuck up your book project from the get-go.

And if you wanna skip the rest of the book after knowing the most common fuckups, eager to finally prioritise your book project, well, mission accomplished! Don't forget to tag me on LinkedIn (@malenebendtsen and #publishingrebel) when you announce you read 20 pages into this book and couldn't stop yourself from finally getting started ;)

So here is the list:

Fuckup #1

Postponing your book to next year. You won't have time next year either. And meanwhile, you'll be stuck and annoyed about not progressing how you want to.

Fuckup #2

Postponing making concrete plans on WHEN you'll prioritise the time and escape somewhere to work your ass off on it. Check my website for book writing escapes. It's not uncommon for participants to write a first full draft in a week. They might be puking when I'm not around but I don't think so - they seem to have a blast!

Fuckup #3

Thinking about marketing when you are done writing your book. Marketing comes first and is an ongoing activity for the next 5 years - or until you write a second book which is very likely, according to the pattern I see among my authors. Make the actual launch the smallest part of your strategy. This book is an asset that will pay off far beyond that. And long before the release date too!

Fuckup #4

Going wide when you should go deep. You are looking to become a known authority. If any, only people who already are authorities should write books that target "anyone who works in a company" or "anyone who wants more time". Problems management care about are not the same problems employees care about. Problems with time that busy moms have are not the problems I have with time (anymore). A bigger market is just bigger. It's not better. And when you target a wide audience, your sales conversion rate is likely to lower, because you are now competing with those who are already strong personal brands. Go deep. Not wide.

Fuckup #5

Not having a clear mental image of your final products and not making design choices before you finish your manuscript. Know which formats you'll publish. And don't consider illustrations purely decorative elements. They are elements to enhance learning and make the reader understand or remember your point better. A classic mistake is to not take into consideration if your book can actually be read out loud. If it can't, it will be difficult to create your audiobook (learned that the hard way!). Listening to your book should be a breeze and not feel as complicated as trying to discreetly adjust a wedgie in public before it drives you nuts.

OK. That's five fuckups for you. How many fuckup possibilities can you handle? ;)

Ok, I'll stop. These truly are the most important fuckups.

The Rebel Method:
6 P's of self-publishing

In short, a well-positioned nonfiction book can help you:

- Build credibility in your niche
- Attract your desired customers
- Attract new business partners
- Get paid well for your work
- Get on stages and in front of bigger audiences
- Find your voice and get clear on your messages

You can use the ideas, methods, tools and strategies shared in this book regardless of whether you want to use your book to start a speaking career, become a sought-after keynote speaker, start a business and figure out your core messages, use it as a lead magnet to build an email list, sell memberships, attract course students and/or coaching or consulting clients, share your story and lessons learned, or build a legacy.

The process is the same no matter your goal. What makes this book and the Rebel Method different is that we start the process by making sure you will successfully publish *a book that will be worth your investment in time and money*, meaning the book will help you reach your ultimate goal and take your business or career to the next level.

In a classical approach, marketing is the last step of a 'write, publish, promote' process. One of the key differences in this approach is that we start and end with marketing and put marketing in between too. Strategy is much more important (for achieving what you want to achieve - and actually also for how easy or troublesome your writing process will be) than… any other factor, really. Strategising, positioning and scoping is your first step and once you crack those nuts, the rest will be a lot easier and simply be tasks to execute.

The phases in the Rebel Method are:

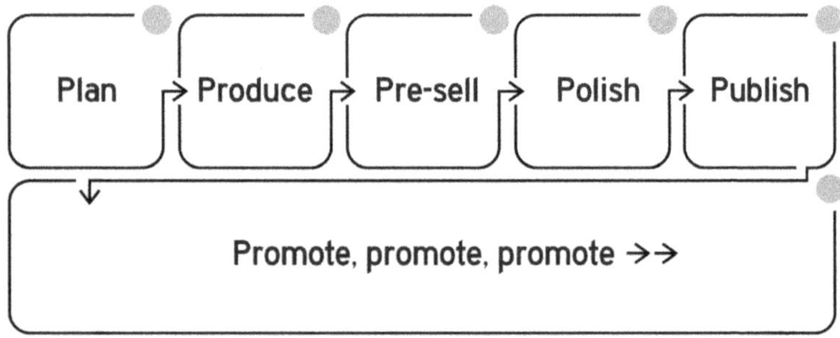

Yeah… you got that right…. I wanted P's only, to help you remember the six phases. I am an MBA, I can't help myself.

But at a meta-level, notice how spending time on putting your recommendations into a system, pretty much also provides a framework for the entire book.

A few things that make the Rebel Method so powerful:

- Three out of six phases are about marketing: Plan, Pre-sell, and Promote

- The creation phase is split in two: Produce and Polish. I will get back to why that is important
- Promote starts from day one

The second part of this book explains each of the 6 Ps:

Planning (Chapter 1) is about positioning your book in the market and knowing how you want the book to fit into and serve your business and personal journey. You'll match that up against how the book will compete in the market, what the exact topic and angle of your book should be, and how your book will be different from other books in the same category. You will also plan how to build an audience for your book and exactly how you will motivate others to promote your book for you.

By and large, the outcome of this process is what you would be asked by any traditional publisher who is considering your book. As a self publisher you'll also need to make sure that the project will be worth it. The Fake Book Proposal is the tangible outcome of this process. It will guide everything you do from here, and ease the writing process.

Producing (Chapter 2) is about outlining your content in detail and creating what I call a first full draft. You will get as quickly as possible to a first version of the entire book, and in a way that will ensure you won't be changing so much later that the nature of the book will change, or that you'll need to rewrite the whole thing. Front-loading decisions are our tool to significantly shorten the time needed to create a powerful manuscript.

Pre-selling (Chapter 3) means selling your book before it's ready to get published, collecting pre-orders. You can start doing that months ahead of the release date. What you need to have ready is a basic manuscript so your content isn't 'moving'. You must know exactly what you are selling. Apart from that, you need the title, the subtitle, the author's name, and a book cover. Possibly a super simple landing page. That's it.

Some authors skip this step (or more or less skip marketing altogether except for the launch party). They are missing out on the best proof there is to know your book will be successful: People paying for your book! Also, they will be paying you money that you can direct back into your book promotion. But most importantly, and this is the main reason we do this, you get to talk about your book months before it comes out which makes it a lot easier to create buzz for your book. Usually, this activity gets you into so many conversations that your overall sales will spike for that reason alone. It's also mandatory to hit bestseller lists.

Polishing (Chapter 4) includes both editing and completing the manuscript, creating the visuals, and designing a beautiful layout of each page that matches your cover. It also includes polishing your launch and marketing campaign, preparing powerful metadata to position your book and making it attractive to both readers, book stores and promotion partners.

Publishing (Chapter 5) includes a few things only: Hitting the button on your self-publishing platform. Or if you choose to distribute physical books, making them available for ongoing fulfilment. Deliver books to people who pre-ordered from your website. To celebrate with your besties. This part of the book explains what self-publishing is, who it's right for and how it's different from traditional publishing. You'll also learn about digital formats: ebook, audiobook, and NFTs. While publishing obviously happens after polishing, you really should read this chapter before Chapter 3 about pre-selling.

Promoting (Chapter 6) your book is the marketing marathon that begins on day one, increases up to your launch and during the pre-sell phase, and stretches for the long haul thereafter. It never ends. There are endless opportunities to promote your book. I dive into some of them in this book. I've also added a bonus section with extraordinary strategies I've come across, to inspire you to do more and go beyond 'traditional'. You'll find those in the Fandango section.

The
PATH

From Idea to Published Author

AUTHORITY

plan 1

Scoping Voyage to Victory

How do you plan to Eiffel-tower the competition with an outstanding book? Are you going to quantum-leap into a new genre for a daring adventure? Will you maintain a laser-beamed focus on one narrow theme, or more broadly present different aspects? Will you chess-master the strategic storytelling and make your book case-heavy? Will you present moon-landing-researched content? Or is it a more spiritual book or a personal story in which you will tattoo your soul onto the pages?

Who is the book for? Which problem do you want to solve? Who else solves the problem? Who will help you sell it? Which formats will you offer? And what does your book funnel look like?

These are all questions you should know the answers to before writing a single word. They will shape your book structure, your writing style, your writing strategy, your marketing, your goals, everything.

What and how much do people read?

Despite blockages worldwide interfering with the delivery of printed books during Covid, sales went just one way: Up. In fact, all age groups read more than ever. The only exception is the 65+ year segment which has stagnated.

And it's not just due to Covid. People, in general, read more books than ever.

At a global level, the book publishing market is expected to have a valuation of $143.65 billion in 2023 and to grow to $163.89 billion by 2030, a 14% increase.

US book sales revenue[6] amounted to 9.1 billion US dollars in 2022[7], a 5.2% decrease from 2021, but still 5.8% above the 2020 level. For the first time, paperbacks surpassed hardbacks, a pattern which might be rooted in the economic downturn and financial hardship many Americans suffer.

Since 2020, the US book market experienced:

- 23% increase in paperbacks
- 24% increase in downloaded audio
- 6% drop in hardbacks

Reconsidering an audio version now? You should. Especially since digital formats are more profitable. You might even want to make the audio version the star of the show. Even though audio is still a much smaller part of book sales, I don't think I need to convince you that audio is the future.

In the UK, book sales increased by 3% in 2022, reaching 6.9 billion GBP[8]. From 2021 to 2022, the UK book market experienced:

- 1-2% decrease in print books
- 8% increase in downloaded audio[9]

Also in the UK market, audiobook download sales growth is significant. Revenue has more than doubled since 2018. Additionally, e-book sales revenue in the United Kingdom climbed by almost 19% in a decade[10].

In general, statistics for e-book sales are sluggish due to how publishers measure sales. But even though audiobooks are poised to overtake ebooks, there is, without a doubt, a significant part of your audience who will prefer the ebook format.

Print is still by far the best selling format. Don't skip the hardback. It generally accounts for 30-35% of total trade sales[11] and it's really no extra work when you are a self publisher, especially if you PoD publish (see Chapter 5).

In fact, you should offer all book formats, print and digital.

Publishing in as many formats as possible helps to convince the algorithm that you are a legit author and publisher, and it helps you serve as many subsegments in your niche as possible, meeting their needs no matter their book consumption preferences. If a person's preferred format isn't available, it's often a reason not to buy, aka lost royalty, lost ranking, and a possibly lost lead.

People obviously love books more than ever. But is this development also true for adult nonfiction books? Yes. The global nonfiction book market is projected to have a 5.7% growth compared to 2021, of which 55.3% is generated in the US[12].

In the US, nonfiction print books account for 45.5% of book sales[13]. According to Penguin Random House, adult nonfiction trade revenue unit sales surpassed fiction revenue already back in 2014. By 2017, nonfiction sales were 35% higher than fiction.[14] Nonfiction is growing, and fast.

> **Fun fact**
>
> *In a 2015 study[15] honouring International Women's Day, FicShelf ranked almost 230 of the bestselling fiction and nonfiction self published titles, and 81% were by women. This compares with the top 100 traditionally published titles on Amazon, of which FicShelf discovered that 61% are written by men.*

Calculating bestseller ROIs

As a business-savvy person, I am sure you know you should consider the return on your investment, in time and money (ROI). But I also suspect that you don't really care about the (income from) book sales and that you are aware of the much bigger potential at the backend of your book funnel. There are some pitfalls you should know about though, so don't skip this section even if that sounds like you.

The average nonfiction author sells 400 books in the first year[16]. This number might shock you or demotivate you,

"

In fact, you should offer all book formats, *print and digital.*

but hear me out because there is good news too. Very good news:

It doesn't really matter.

Firstly, you are not average and you are not the kind of person who will 'forget' to have a proper marketing plan. You are a business person first, a marketer of your knowledge, not a hobby writer. And even if you strategically decide, simply having a book is enough and other projects take priority, you will still experience the authority effect.

Secondly, the most successful authors make loads of money from their books - even if not on the book itself. Let's dive into that for a minute.

Recently, I was bombarded on all channels with ads for a book on how to sell. The book was free, I just had to pay $6.95 for them to ship it to me. The cost of printing, storing and sending the book is likely to dilute profit or even result in a loss for each person taking the offer.

Yet, they are making loads of money on that offer.

I will get back to how in a minute and tell you the rest of the story. But first some more depressing news.

Amazon and others will tell you that your royalties as a self published author are anything from 35-70%. This is true, especially for e-books. Audiobooks are often at 70-80%.

We really shouldn't call it royalties but your profit margin, when you are a self publisher. Royalty is a term that expresses the payment you'll get from selling the rights to your book to a publisher (yep, you'll sell the rights).

Some will compare that profit margin to the royalty you can receive as a traditionally published author which might be 10-15% for a hardback book and 7-8% for a paperback. For audio and ebooks, usually around 25%[17], but I've seen contracts with the same rate for all formats.

So self publishing sounds appealing for that reason alone.

But be aware, because it's not an accurate picture to paint and it's not the reality for all print books.

Let's do the math so we make sure you know the pitfalls to watch out for.

If you want to publish a 200-page paperback, black and white print only, on white paper, via Amazon KDP, and price it at $15, your royalties per book will be $5.60 or 37.3%. So far so good.

However, if you want to publish the same book with standard coloured pages, your royalty will drop to $2.60. Paperbacks printed in standard colour have a matte finish. If you need more sharpness and richness of colour, you'll need premium colour print. In that case, you'll need to set your market price at $24 to break even with only $0.40 in royalties per book.

If you want it in colours and hardback, you are up to $32 to break even.

A hardcover, black and white only, priced at $14 will also break even.

10% royalties from a traditionally published book with a retail price of $15 is also just $1.50. For the paperback even lower. This type of royalty is called retail royalties or list royalties and is based on the list price. Sometimes royalties are calculated on net sales prices - meaning you are partly financing the discounts the publisher may agree to when negotiating with major book outlets.

Also, be aware that an advance is exactly what the word says. You are receiving money upfront instead of after the sales and you'll only receive royalties after you paid the advance back with the royalties you earn from the book.

And there is a couple of things more, you should also know:

You'll have to wait longer for your money. Publishers often pay royalties twice a year based on sales that took place during the preceding half-calendar year. So, sales from January-June are paid in October.

Almost all books are sold on a returnable basis - if they don't sell, the bookstore can return them for full credit. Roughly 20% of royalties are withheld by the publisher pending book returns.

Anyways…

Before we return to the story, perhaps you'd like to know how you can increase your profit margin and avoid ending up being forced to charge too much for your book due to insane print costs.

I am now assuming, you choose to become a self publishing author using a PoD strategy (see Chapter 5), publishing with Amazon KDP, for example, but the principles are the same.

In order to lower your print cost, you should:

1. **Make your book shorter**

    Fewer pages means lower print cost. That can be ok if you can get your message across on fewer pages. A great example of successfully doing this is the widely popular book 'This book will teach you how to write better' by Neville Medhora which is only 54 pages long. Longer is not better. Don't waste your readers' time with fluff. Just give them the good stuff.

2. **Avoid using colours inside your book**

    There are many ways to create a beautiful design using only a greyscale. Or even just black and white. Using graphical elements, including illustrative drawings, boxing in important takeaways, using big water-marks on a page, etc, you can create a great book without colours. Some platforms will allow you only to pay for the coloured pages, but on Amazon KDP, so far it's all or nothing.

There is a lot more to be said on this topic and Amazon KDP is not your only publishing option. My point right now is that you will probably not get rich from selling books:

- Paperback of 200 pages
- Optimised on the above parameters (black/white)
- Selling the industry average amount of books
- Royalty: $5.75*400 copies = $2.300

Now, if writing books is a hobby that's enough for something nice for your family.

But as a business person, counting the work hours that go into generating that revenue, it really makes no sense.

So why do people do it anyway?

Because of the backend.

Up until this point, I made no differentiation between publishing fiction and nonfiction. As a nonfiction author with a teaching business or a speaking career or similar, your calculation is a lot more advanced.

In fact, there is little comparison.

Your goal is not to sell books. Your goal is to distribute books to the right audience who are interested in what you are selling in your business.

This brings me back to the story about the '$6.95 for shipping' offer. I had never heard about the author before. I had never heard about the book before.

Did I take the offer? Yes.

Why? Because it seemed legit and I'd like to continue my education on selling. It was a great video ad that caught my attention.

Here is what the process looked like:

1. I saw the video ad: Free book for $6.95 shipping
2. Clicked to order the book
3. There was a new offer for $37 dollars to get the audio version + 7 in-depth reports on topics that seemed very relevant to me.
4. When responding no thank you to this, there was a new small offer which I took for $27.

Let's use this as an example to calculate what it could look like for you - with the industry average book sales (which you can easily exceed):

1. 400 people take the free book but pay $7 for shipping. Let's say your total cost is $10 per book (print, shipping and handling). You will then have a loss of $3 per book, $1,200 in total.

"Your goal is not to sell books. Your goal is to distribute books to the **right audience** *who are* **interested** *in what you are selling in your business.*

2. 10% take you up on the 37 offer, resulting in a $1,480 revenue. Your net income is now positive, $280.

3. Of the 90% who didn't take the $37 offer, 10% take the $27 offer, adding $972 to your profit which now has a total of $1,252 (or $3.13 per book).

Now, this may seem like a lot of work to earn $1,252.

But…

You also added 400 people to your email list.

When selling via bookstores online or offline, buyers remain anonymous to you and can only convert them to email subscribers if they read your book (or some of it) and take your offer of more helpful content on your website. If they order a free book from your website, you'll get their email addresses.

Also note, 76 of the 400 people are highly targeted leads (40 people taking the $37 offer and 36 people taking the $27 offer). They are buyers who are already invested in their education and in solving the problem you can help them solve.

Imagine if 5 of them purchased your $997 program either immediately or later. This will bring your book revenue from 400 free books up to $6.237 or $15.60 per book.

Now, that's a lot more fun.

On top of that, 2 people might ask for individual coaching. Another 2 people might ask you to speak at their event. They are happy to purchase 400 copies of your book as a gift to the audience.

Do you see where this is going?

Whether you sell 100 copies, 5,000 copies or 400 copies, the book is just the trigger of something bigger.

Oh…wait!

Let me put that in a box so you never forget:

> Your book is just the trigger of something bigger!

Bestselling nonfiction authors have three things in common:

- They have a **profit plan** and know how the book will make them money before they start writing
- They solve a specific problem or cater to a specific pain point and have a clear **content strategy**
- They have a **book promotion** plan and know how people will hear about the book

In other words, successful nonfiction authors have a common view of the ROLE the book plays in their business, and in the journey of the customer.

"
Your book is just the **trigger** *of* something bigger!

They don't sell books.

They sell a story of transformation.

They sell the idea that transformation is possible. The dream can come true. The pain can go away. The goal can be achieved.

Successful authors teach to *remove the knowledge gaps, remove possible objections, and feed the desire to transform*. A great nonfiction book educates the reader and builds trust in the author's expertise or wisdom, and the purpose is to **motivate the reader** to **pursue the result** they desire.

The best nonfiction authors manage to draw a certain amount of readers into their sales funnels and offer the next step in a compelling way. Their book is a marketing tool. Not a product. They might profit less from the book but have a solid, highly profitable backend. They know their numbers.

A **backend** is a business system in which the author offers products or services in a carefully designed order.

Ideally, you would have at least one highly scalable product available so you can grow your business limitlessly. It can be a smaller "no-brainer" product - a product that I would be stupid not to purchase with the book. Or it could be a higher ticket product. The important thing is, your maximum revenue isn't defined by how many hours a day has.

" *Successful authors teach to remove the* knowledge gaps, *remove possible objections, and* feed the desire *to transform.*

Here are some ideas for what you could sell at the backend of your book:

- Keynotes
- Expert talks
- Coaching programs
- Digital courses
- Memberships
- Masterminds
- Workshops
- Event tickets
- Consulting
- Software / apps

You can also publish a nonfiction book to differentiate yourself in other service niches, or even from other brick and mortar businesses. As long as you solve one of the 3 kinds of problems people generally have (which I will share later), you can pull readers closer to your business with a nonfiction book.

And hey!

You are writing this book anyway, right? Why leave money on the table instead of having a more strategic approach with close to limitless potential? Knowing what you want people to do next defines what content should go into the book.

Positioning your book for success

I am aware that talking about the WHY behind your business may seem a little off track. However, in my experience, writing a book often leads to a process of becoming even more clear on what you want in your business. Knowing what you want in your business is a prerequisite to being able to produce a book that will attract the right people to your business. It is also the best way to avoid the pitfall of accidentally writing a book for yesterday's business and not where you want to go.

Who is the book supposed to attract to your business? Throughout my career, I have been stunned by how common it is that business owners lack clarity on which customers are the most profitable to them - and even which customers they prefer serving or are able to serve the best.

I am sure that's not you, but when I ask authors to define their target reader, it is more common than not that the answer is very long and usually starts with "well, it can be relevant for both x, y, and z". While it is wonderful if there is a huge market for your book, the probability of success diminishes at the same pace as you increase the size of your target market

- Your target reader should be the person who is the *perfect* customer for your most profitable product
- The perfect customer is the person you can provide the most *value* to with the least amount of effort

- The least amount of effort comes down to what and how you need to teach - and your skills and *desire* to do so

In other words, your book should attract the person you can help the most while enjoying it and loving your business.

Whether you want to use your book to start or grow a business, to start a speaking career or something else, knowing exactly who you want to attract and why you will love serving them is essential to both your book and business success.

Diving deep into how to discover your why is not the purpose of this book. Getting you passionate about fulfilling your purpose with your book is the purpose of this book so let me just briefly share a few inspiring stories and concepts that might help you get some direction for which book you should write. You will see how these authors' lives or business purposes (or both) are reflected in the category of the books they authored.

> **Hal Elrod** was dead for 6 minutes at a young age and has since been dedicated to helping people get the most out of life. His book 'Miracle Morning' shares a life-hacking morning routine which has a tremendous impact on people's daily habits. Miracle Morning is a great example of how changing people's habits can snowball your book to the top of bestseller lists. This book is promoted as much by readers as by the author. With this book, Hal has started a movement toward

people living better lives. A purpose that is very close to his heart.

Brendon Burchard was suicidal at the age of 19 and suffered from serious depression after losing his girl-friend whom he loved deeply. This led to a car accident in which he nearly lost his life. Upon this experience, he asked himself three questions: Have I lived? Have I loved? Did I matter? These questions are today at the core of Brendon's business, and his books about high performance habits are related to having meaningful goals and a positive mindset.

Mel Robbins hit rock bottom and nearly lost every-thing she cared about in life. Her anxiety was so bad, she could barely drag herself out of bed. 'The Five Second Rule', her simple tool, backed by research, has changed the lives of millions. Her TED Talk is in the top 20 of most-watched TED Talks, of all time.

Mark Manson was a bit of a player, was broke, root-lessly travelled the world for 5 years, suffered depression after losing his best friend, and had an insane stalker for years. His writing is controversial and flies in the face of conventional self-help advice. His colourful language packs a punch as suggested by the titles of his books 'The Subtle Art of Not Giving a F*ck' and 'Everything is fucked'. As of the end of June 2023, the first book has spent 297 weeks on the New York Times Bestseller list.

These authors are in the self-help/personal transformation space. Their books (and businesses) are centred around changing habits and the benefits and impact of having a positive, confident and/or self-appreciative mindset. They are books in the HAPPINESS category, an area the authors struggled with themselves. Their purpose is to share the lessons they learned so others can live better and happier lives. Their work is also a daily reminder to themselves to live their best lives.

HAPPINESS is one of four main categories for nonfiction books. The three others are HEALTH, WEALTH, and TIME. Almost any book fits into one of these and some fit into more than one. Brendon Burchard's book 'High Performance' is, for example, also in the WEALTH category (Business & Money, personal finance)

Let's take a look at some other examples of books in the WEALTH category:

> **Pat Flynn** was laid off from his job as an architect during the economic collapse in 2008. He had to find a way to make money online fast to support his family. He started a blog sharing what he learned. He later published 'Smart Passive Income', 'Will It fly?', and 'Superfans'.

> **Robert Kiyosaki** grew up with two paternal influences. His own father and the father of his friend. He noticed the differences in how the two dads talked about and dealt with money. His book 'Rich Dad, Poor Dad' shares

how to become financially free. He teaches finances so a 9-year-old can understand, just like he could when Rich Dad taught him about money and investments.

Emma Due Blitz, Camilla Falkenberg, and Anna Sophie Hartvigsen, three young Danish ladies from my hood, all began investing as teenagers despite coming from backgrounds where nobody talks about money and investing. They are on a mission to close the financial gender gap, teaching women to invest. Their book 'Girls just wanna have funds' is being endorsed by Hillary Clinton. Yes, I am a little proud of them ;)

In the HEALTH category, we find authors who struggled with either body or mental issues.

Arianna Huffington collapsed from sleep deprivation, breaking her cheekbone in the fall. She dived into deep research on the subject and her book 'Sleep Revolution' includes 1,200 references to research. It's also worth mentioning that her website Huffington Post was the first digital media company to win a Pulitzer.

Of course, we also find books by healthcare professionals in this category.

Ok, I am gonna speed this up, because I think you got the point. The TIME category includes examples like:

Brian Tracy
'Eat That Frog!: 21 Great Ways to Stop Procrastinating and Get More Done in Less Time'

Tim Ferris

'The 4-hour Workweek: Escape 9-5, Live Anywhere, and Join the New Rich'

David Allen

'Getting Things Done: The Art of Stress-Free Productivity'

Greg McKeown

'Essentialism: The Disciplined Pursuit of Less'

Gary W. Keller and **Jay Papasan**

'The ONE Thing: The Surprisingly Simple Truth About Extraordinary Results'

Daniel Pink

'When: The Scientific Secrets of Perfect Timing'

So to which category does this book belong then?

Malene Bendtsen

'How to Become Nonfiction Author: Tips to Writing & Self Publishing a Book Without Losing Your F*cking Mind'

Well, in fact, it's a great example of how a book can fit into several categories. It's also a great example of how choosing a category will shape the angle of your book.

I could have chosen:

- Happiness - How to leave a legacy or have a bigger impact in the world with a book (meaning) - not what I chose to focus on

- Health - Not so much - unless we count keeping you sane while writing ;)
- Wealth - How to make more money with a book
- Time - How to write and publish a book faster

This book is primarily a TIME book. You are a busy business person and I know time is the biggest obstacle you have to overcome to become a published author. It also falls into the WEALTH category because being financially better off is the ultimate goal you are hoping to achieve, publishing a nonfiction book. Also, because time is a constraint, and you need to invest time to become an author, it has to be worth it.

Do you see how choosing a category forced me to go through a process of reasoning and positioning the book not only in terms of metadata (which categories to add when publishing it) but in terms of your goal?

It's ok if your book fits into more than one category. The important thing is that you put some thought behind which book you write. And you need to go deeper than this too. A broad topic is not specific enough to help you stay on track when you start creating your book. You need boundaries for what you will and will not give space to in your book. And yep, it's more common to have too much to say than too little once you start writing.

Another thing I urge you to do is to take just a little time to consider if the big promise in your book matches the big

"Choosing a category will shape the angle of your book.

promise you made to yourself. Are you writing a book that will shape your future the way you want it to?

Here is a quick way to do a reality check on that based on my own story.

In the summer of 2021, I travelled for 10 weeks in Spain and Portugal. A 10,000 km (or 6,200 miles) road trip all the way around the Iberian Peninsula. You can get a lot of thinking done during that time and I had a long list of audiobooks ready to inspire my thinking.

One of them was Simon Sinek's 'Find your why'. Simon recommends a 7-step process of why's which I used something like this as I drove all the way from Denmark to Gibraltar with pit stops to take notes and complete each step, writing down my why's:

- Why do you have your business?
- Why?
- Why?
- Why?
- Why?
- Why?
- Why?

Did you just count if there really were seven? ;)

Keep your answers short and concise. Just one or two sentences. Dive deep into emotions and be honest with yourself until you reach the last step seven levels down.

I was quite surprised to discover that the real reason behind my WHY is a strong desire to free people from other people's ideas of who they are or how they should want to live their life so they can fully be who they truly are. Not what they are supposed to be or how they want to be. What they ARE. I strongly believe we are put in this world to live our fullest potential and we can only do that if we don't allow ourselves to be stopped from being who we really are.

Once you are clear on your seven levels of WHY, ask yourself these 4 questions:

1. Why are you on this planet?
2. How are you living your purpose?
3. What do you 'happen' to do?
4. Why do you want to publish a book?

To help you understand how this works, here is mine:

Why are you on this planet	I am here to facilitate the spreading of knowledge and education so we can all live our full potential
How are you living your purpose	I am a teacher using a cascade model for bigger impact
What do you 'happen' to do?	I teach selfpublishing nonfiction books to solopreneurs with a teaching or coaching business
Why do you want to publish a book?	To remove obstacles keeping you from contributing to my end goal: that all have access to growing and learning

Knowing this has helped me write this book. I am here to help you live YOUR full potential - but also help you impact the lives of as many other people as possible through your most value-generating products, your backend.

This is why the focus of this book is on how to make your book the RIGHT book for you personally and for your business. It could have focused a lot more on technicalities (no worries, there is that too in this book), or I could have gone into even more detail in the more practical steps.

THIS book, however, is the book that best:

1. **Fit my WHY**
    Therefore it is worth spending time making it a great and helpful book. It makes me feel inspired to finish the book and promote the heck out of it so it can help more people.

2. **Help aspiring authors reach their END goal**
    Because it teaches a book system - not just how to write a book but how to know which book will have the biggest impact - on your audience and your bank account.

3. **Make you believe you can**
    Because I help you build a super solid plan to set you up for the level and kind of success you want, aka it is worth your time.

4. **Will build rapport between you and me**
    Or at least give me a chance to win your trust if you are my perfect customer. Hopefully, you will feel the real me and how I am not just an information provider but a potential guide on your journey to author success.

If you exchange number two with your target readers' end goal, you'll see these four criteria should fit your book as well.

* * *

You should also research and decide the scope of your target audience. How narrowly should you define the audience for your book? Your niche might be small and potent because people in it are eager to invest in a solution that is currently not available or designed specifically for them.

Or it might be gigantic and you should in fact consider narrowing your target group and find a segment that is currently underserved so you can have a stronger position in the competition.

You are looking for a HUNGRY and resourceful niche that will be able to pay for your backend services. This really is no different than strategising for your business and we are not going to dive deep into this. Just do a quick check-in with yourself if you are going too broad and making it more difficult for yourself to compete in a very competitive market.

I am sure you also see that I am bringing this up because the scope of your audience will shape the content and even the book title.

Here are some examples to inspire you - most of them from successful authors of mine:

COMPETITIVE	LESS	EVEN LESS
Leadership	High-performance teams	Creating meaningful jobs for young employees
Marketing	Social media	TikTok advertising for small businesses
Stress relief	Yoga	Restorative yoga
Creativity	Crafts	Embroidery
Sales	Export	Export US-EU
Change Management	Agile development	Managing agile teams
Parenting	Motherhood	Raising kids like a Viking mom

Targeting a subsegment may result in primarily two things:

- More depth in your book (aka more value)
- Easier to recognise that the book is exactly right for your target reader

It might even be easier to attract people from other subsegments. I might be interested in learning about Nordic parenting even if I am a dad and not a mom, or trying restorative yoga even if I usually practise a different discipline. Or try embroidery if I am usually a knitter.

Too broad of a topic is easily overwhelming to you as a writer, creating an unnecessary risk of getting lost in your manuscript. You are also at risk of overwhelming the reader - and it makes the book more difficult to compete. If you have an enormous amount of content to share, write two books instead.

On a side note: This is one of the areas where self publishing is an advantage. Traditional publishers favour mass markets to secure their margins and might want you to go broader also in your content. But that's really not in your interest when you are looking to be the king or queen of a specific niche. When you speak to 'average' you are speaking to no one and that lowers your sales conversion rate.

Only if you already have a large marketing platform, meaning thousands and thousands of followers, email subscribers, customers and a strong industry network, do I recommend you go for a broader niche.

This is not a fame game, it's smart marketing and ROI management.

* * *

You also need to look at the **competition**. Become clear on how your book is *different*. How is it even more helpful to your perfect customer? How is it different in terms of readability and visual appearance? Which language style will it be? Does your book come with perks?

Examples of how your book can be different:

- Narrower - only looks at....
- Broader - looks at all of...
- Based on my own research in the specific niche
- Has a lot more examples
- Looks at top management instead of entrepreneurs
- Looks at the problem from a biological perspective instead of ....
- It's shorter and focuses on tools
- It's for employees, not management
- It's for men and has a masculine vibe
- It's funnier
- More professional design
- The design tells a story in itself
- Easier to read and re-read
- Not a textbook but explained in drawings
- It fits into a pocket
- It's implementation focused not just describing what to do
- It has dedicated space to do the work while reading
- There is a complimentary workbook available
- It's a planner

Also consider how long your book should be. What would your perfect customer prefer? I can tell you that they might be *impressed* by a very solid 400-page book, but they might not read it.

Here are a few things to guide you:

- If you are self publishing using print-on-demand (Chapter 5), you'll want it below 250 pages for cost reasons, even 200 pages.
- Amazon requires a minimum of 24 pages for a paperback book and 75 pages for a hardback.
- You'll need 110 pages for a proper spine with readable text on it.
- Longer is not better. Some of the all-time bestselling books are just around 100 pages.

While researching competitors' books, also do this:

- Screenshot the covers so your designer can see what you are up against
- Note prices, number of pages and available formats (what is the audience used to and how can you differ?)
- Which words are used in the description? If the book is ranking high on Amazon there is a good chance some of these words are keywords that can provide traffic to your book details page and convert visitors to buyers

All of this will help you nail your book topic, angle and what your end product will look like.

WHAT IS THE CATEGORY OF YOUR BOOK?

Overall category

- ☐ Health (body, mind, soul)
- ☐ Weath (make money, invest, save money)
- ☐ Happiness (relationships, self-love, meaning)
- ☐ Time (antistress, productivity)

Subcategory:

Can you be even more specific?

DIFFERENTIATING FACTORS

My book is like ________________________________
________________ [strong authority piece in your niche]

but is different ________________________________
_____ ________________________________ [in what
way?]

The book you compare to can be a competing book. It can also be the *style* of the book (noncompeting book in a different category) that's going to be similar.

WHAT WILL A BOOK DO FOR YOUR BUSINESS?

Start a speaking career

- ☐ Raise your credibility
- ☐ Get paid for speaking
- ☐ Enjoy profitable on-site book sales
- ☐ Send something to event managers when pitching

Become a sought-after keynote speaker

- ☐ Raise your fees (it's not uncommon to double)
- ☐ Well-known expert in your niche
- ☐ New stages if a visionary book with a big new idea
- ☐ Capture leads without being salesy

Start a business and figure out your core messages

- ☐ Use the process to figure out or refine your message
- ☐ Develop key concepts and models to teach
- ☐ Build your audience from the get-go with freebies to test the interest and value for your audience
- ☐ Create engagement and responsiveness involving your audience in an exciting book project

Build your email list

- ☐ Let cold audiences learn about you and your ideas
- ☐ Use your book as a giveaway (freebie)
- ☐ Create strong incentive to visit your website
- ☐ Add highly targeted subscribers to your email list

Attract course students or coaching / consulting clients

- ☐ Educate the reader to be able to decide their path
- ☐ Make prospects emotionally ready to invest in change
- ☐ Feed the dream of a brighter future
- ☐ Position yourself as a guide on their change journey

Share your story and lessons learned

- ☐ Help others who experience a pain you know too well
- ☐ Get the story of your chest and process the pain
- ☐ Inspire others to tell their story
- ☐ Transform pain into a teachable business concept

Raise authority

- ☐ Hit NYT (and other) bestseller lists…
- ☐ Rank at the top of Amazon category list
- ☐ Have articles published in industry magazines
- ☐ …. What is important to you?

FAKE BOOK PROPOSAL

The 3 cornerstones of your marketing plan

Before you even start writing your book, you must have some idea of how you will promote it. Too often I see aspiring authors have no plan of how to reach their potential readers. And I am not only suggesting you start planning but also that you act on certain parts of your marketing plan. You don't need to be specific about all parts of your marketing plan yet, but having these three different plans thought through at an overall level is highly beneficial.

The **Audience Growth Plan** includes how you will warm up your existing audience and make them eager to buy your book and even help you promote it.

It also includes:

- How will you expand your current audience? Will you rely on organic marketing, creating a freebie, or being a podcast guest? Or will you rely on running ads to increase your email list?

- How will you engage your social media audience and involve customers or members in the process of creating the book?

The people who show an active interest in the book will make up a very targeted email list. These are high-quality leads. Figure out how to add tags to these people wherever you capture the lead.

You can use this list in several ways:

- If there are enough of them, you'll be able to upload them as a list to your ads platform and let the platform find more people with similar profiles to show your ads to.

- You can also build an actual launch team with people who are willing to commit to helping you promote your book. Maybe you'll invite them all to an online launch party with fun things happening they don't want to miss. Ask them for reviews on Amazon. Or ask them who they know who can be helpful in your book launch.

The **Network Expansion Plan** includes thinking through how you can make your book an addition to somebody else's work so you can get access to collaboration opportunities. How can you incentivise people with similar audiences to become affiliates for your book? I know, sharing the profits from the book may seem like an unnecessary cost. But think again. If you designed a proper book funnel, as I described in 'Calculating your ROI', the value of each purchase will be much higher than simply the royalties. So who has similar audiences to yours, and which of them would recognise whatever you are an expert at, as bringing *additional value* to their audience? Value that they are not able to provide themselves, or can't do as great as you can? For example, anyone who teaches how to create a great keynote is very likely to have an audience interested also in my book services or private membership. What would that look like for you?

While you are still in the process of writing your book, you can start providing value to these potential new partners. Build friendships and relationships over time so that when you are ready to launch, they'd be willing to help you with your promotion. Can you create some bonus that only the listeners on their podcast would receive when they order a book during your pre-order phase? Could you create a small course to complement the book to either give as a bonus or to add to your book funnel, so that the collaboration partner would get a share of the *total sales from the book and the course?*

Who you want to deepen or create new relationships with, and how you plan to incentivise them during the launch, are great questions to answer at this early stage. Your book is not a stand-alone product. It's part of the system that makes up your future book-based teaching empire. Have a plan for how you can tap into other people's already lukewarm audiences (because they know that person if not you) in a way that benefits all parties.

The **Amazon Ranking Plan** is all about cold audiences. Getting visibility for your book and getting it in front of people who might never have heard about you. As a nonfiction author, you can't skip Amazon altogether, unless you have a strong vendetta against their domination and are willing to sacrifice a chunk of your book sales. Your book should be available on Amazon. End of story.

However, how much emphasis you should put on the ranking of your book in online bookstores, including Amazon, depends on your strategy and how you want to distribute your marketing efforts and budget. The surprising fact is that in many cases reaching number one in your category is not difficult if you know how to pick the right category. Staying number one is much more difficult, and requires constant traffic to your book details page and a good conversion rate, meaning those who see your book also buy it.

You don't need a specific plan for creating the necessary amount of traffic yet. But you should consider whether it's even an important sales channel for you, or if being on

Amazon is merely to be able to have a place to send individuals to occasionally, and for being able to add credibility since people tend to be impressed by the fact that your book is there. If you plan to primarily sell your book B2B, to bigger organisations, as part of your consultancy or training services, or you will primarily sell it as a part of your offer to those who host events where you will be a speaker, well, then the effort you need to make to rank on Amazon over time, may simply not be worth it.

On the other hand, if ranking well on Amazon is important to you, you'll need to create traffic from other places (like podcasts or ads) to the book details page yourself, you need the details page to convert well, and you need reviews. Lots of reviews. You'll also need the right metadata, and you'll need to use them correctly for the algorithm to understand who to show your book to.

And that brings me to the reason why this is part of the planning phase. Letting your work be guided by non-competitive keywords and adding those keywords to your subtitle and perhaps even your title can be what makes or breaks your ranking strategy.

A great example of the importance of this is one of my authors who wanted my help in editing and publishing her book. The book was about Urban Survival. During the keyword research, I discovered that there was a lot of search for the term "urban survival *planner*" - but no one used that search term and none of the books in the relevant categories were actually planners.

We decided to adjust the manuscript and turn the book into a planner. In other words, knowing this at an early stage helped us tap into a much more specific need and gain a lot more visibility in a crowded spot. In this case, the book had already been published in another language with a publisher and the manuscript was merely a translation. Had this author known about this possibility before writing, a lot of the later work adjusting it could have been avoided, assuming readers have the same need in both countries.

The takeaway here is that keyword research can reveal needs that should influence the content of your book. On the other hand, I am also saying that if Amazon is not a significant sales channel, and you already have lots of experience with the customers you are planning to sell the book to, then keywords may not matter at all.

Either way, you should plan how you want to sell your book *at an overall level* from the get-go and let that shape your strategy. You will, for example, not get any customer data from Amazon about who bought your book. So what is your plan to convert readers to buyers if Amazon is your main channel?

What will you tease in the book that they need to go to your website to get? And how will you incentivise collaboration partners if there is no other funnel than Amazon?

This is all part of your book strategy. Thinking this through is paramount to author success.

Can you guess which non-competitive keywords *I included on the* cover of this book?

Do your keyword research early and find relevant keywords that a large number of people actually type into the search bar, but where the books shown on the search results page are not selling well. If your book is more closely matched with the keywords (in your title, subtitle, description and added as metadata), and a higher number of people actually purchase your book, Amazon will rank you up to be at page 1 and eventually rank your book as number 1 for those search terms.

produce

2

First Draft Dash-o-thon

The fastest path to a high-quality book requires two things:

1. A solid picture of what goes into the book and not
2. Eliminating yourself as the roadblock

It's pretty darn motivating having a first version of your script. You are far less likely to stop yourself from moving forward once your ideas have become tangible in your manuscript. This in itself is reason enough to power through and get to a *first full draft* as quickly as humanly possible.

As a benefit, you are now able to hire someone else to finish editing your script. I am not saying you necessarily should. But you could if time is your biggest constraint. You can get to the finish line even if you need help with your manuscript or simply want to move faster, spending less time. If half of your content is still in your head and not on paper, no one can help.

Another factor at play is that when you move too slowly, sh*t happens. Life happens. Customers happen. Christmas happens. Writing an hour here and there, or even a day here and there, simply is not an effective strategy. You end up spending half the time re-reading, re-thinking and re-writing. And all of those extra hours are hours you can't invoice to anyone.

" *If half of your content is still* in your head *and* not on paper, *no one can help.*

You won't ever really have time. To efficiently write a book you need to make it **your only priority** - but for a short while. It is after all your most important business project. Not a hobby project. For a while, consider your business and your personal aspirations as your most important customer.

I want you to realise, we are not taking years or months to get to this stage. Having a first full draft of your book is 100% possible within weeks, depending on what else is on your schedule. In fact, I am writing this while in Spain hosting a writing camp. The participants are four days in and have most of their content in the first version by now. In all fairness, we properly prepared as prescribed in Chapter 1 before we came. Four days!! I know that's appealing to you since time is a scarce resource.

* * *

Some worry about - right or wrong - if their writing skills are good enough to write a book. I never worry about that when I take on coaching clients. I have what I need in my toolbox to get the gold out of their head and help them elevate the content so the book does exactly what it's supposed to. If that's something you worry about, there are ways to get around that.

On the other hand, there are people who trust their writing abilities too much. They bungee-jump into it and they type and type and type away because they heard someone say the holy grail is writing some specific amount of words per day,

ESC
TO W

APIE
RITE

just letting it flow from your fingertips without any filter or judgement until you have your first rough draft - then rewrite it.

I should love the fact that so many people are given this advice. I've built a great business on helping them out after they failed for the third time and they are stuck on page 50. I mean, like massive-bubblegum-in-your-long-hair-stuck. Using this approach, you are significantly increasing the risk of getting completely lost in your manuscript or losing motivation because you have no idea where or when it's ending. And then Christmas happens. You re-read, re-think, re-write….

Your brain is naturally wired for a different process and it's just sad to think about all of those half-written books, given up upon by incredibly knowledgeable teachers. So I came up with a different and much more effective way to write. A method that tornados through writer's block and creates a path to create a high-quality first full draft as quickly as possible.

How to not let your brain fuck up your writing

Nobody has time to write a book. Nobody with a running business at least. You <u>take</u> time and <u>escape</u>. Boom. To go faster, you either invest bigger chunks of time, invest money for someone to help you out, or work smarter. In a minute,

I will show you how you can **front-load your writing** to have each part of your brain work at its best. If you wanna go faster and have a better result, that's non-negotiable.

But first a word on habits. Because you might not have it as a goal to go faster, even after reading all of my arguments against a slower process. I respect that. But I'd still recommend that you work smarter to get to the first full draft as quickly as possible. Then, if you are usually not project-oriented but prefer a disciplined daily routine, you can shift to that.

I assume this is your first book?

If so, you won't have any experience writing a book. Only stories about how hard it is. That reflects the process *that* person used for his or her book. Your writing style and your writing habits should build on *your* strengths. Yes. Being disciplined is a strength and it will come in handy later.

But for a great start that eliminates much of the time otherwise needed to write your manuscript, what you need is *a solid foundation* and a process that's aligned with *how your brain works*. You need first and foremost to draw on your teaching skills and business skills. And the natural processes of your brain that will either facilitate or fuck up your writing.

My approach is to accept what has been documented to be true and coined as the Pareto rule. Of all the work you need to do, 20% will produce 80% of the value. Or in this case; We accept that the first draft will not be perfect. We are aiming at an 80% complete manuscript in one go, spending only 20% of our time.

This means you will make an effort and use front-loading to ensure you have 80% as an outcome - not 40% or 70%. We aim at the best possible result within the restriction that we only spend 20% of the time and won't bother with nitty-gritty details. We accept imperfection but also push ourselves to properly prepare so an 80% outcome is likely.

Then we hit the discipline button and finish it up so we reach, not 100% but 110%, and create amazing value for the reader and a masterpiece you can be proud of many years on.

But what the heck do you mean by front-loading, Malene?

I am glad you asked.

Front-loading means that we make <u>all</u> (all!) decisions before writing a single word. This helps us be deliberate and strategic about the content so we don't accidentally end up with random content and basically a different book than what we intended to write. This easily happens without front-loading! Random content is for hobby writing - not for business. This book is a strategic asset to use to elevate your business and "random" is unacceptable and very unfortunate.

The problem is that - especially for people like you and me - our right side of the brain is easily triggered and uncon-

To write your manuscript, what you need is a solid foundation *and a process that's aligned with how your brain works.*

trollably gushes new ideas at a pace that sometimes forces us to stay away from normal people so we won't overwhelm them with our crazy thoughts ;)

At the same time, boredom is what we are the least comfortable with (not at all comfortable, actually!) and we'll do anything to escape it. Writing lots and lots of sentences and walls of text does sound super boring, doesn't it? The problem is there is no way around producing text for your book. So how can we ensure the smoothest process?

Your brain <u>will</u> fuck it up for you, if you take a traditional approach, writing top to bottom from a 1-2 page outline of the book. What happens is that even if you are a super fast typer, the creative right side of your brain will have plenty of time to get bored. What happens then? It sees all the beautiful images that your written words also are, and it starts having fun with you. "Hey!, how about if you also included a chapter on this?", "Oh, fun, who said that by the way?", "You know, I know a really good story about that but you should put it in the first chapter instead of the one you randomly chose", "This reminds me, you should make a model people can refer to, wait, that should probably be reflected in the structure of the book", ….

You get the point. To help your creative brain perform at its best and your productive, sequential brain perform at its best, you need to separate the processes of creatively coming up with ideas and making decisions about the content from the actual text production. Which, by the way, is the reason this chapter is named 'production', even though we are not done with the creative part at all yet. I want you to think differently about writing and let go of non-relevant assumptions about writing happening in a certain way. Who cares what Hemingway did? Or your famous auntie who writes poetry? Not relevant. There is a smarter way for nonfiction writing.

The creative part of the process has as the end result that the right side of your brain can place an order for what exactly the left side should produce. This will ensure you end up with a remarkable book that helps the right people get to the right place to turn them into customers and buyers of your most profitable services. Front-loading saves you months and months of time but also usually results in a much stronger book.

However important it is to define the task correctly before writing, I also want to encourage you to only spend days - not weeks or months or even years - on planning your book. You know your sh*t. You teach it already. So let's get cracking!

Our first step is to create some boundaries for your book. You already worked on your positioning in Chapter 1 but we need to go deeper. We do this by asking 4 magical questions:

1. What is **the overall problem** that your book solves?

2. Which **4-7 underlying problems** need to be solved in order for the overall problem to be solved?

To answer these two questions, take a teaching approach and break down what the reader needs to learn or do to get the result they desire - and to become ready to take action and go into the process of solving the problem or living their dream. Your book should fill the gap between where they are at right now, and where you need them to be to connect with your business and immediately or over time to become a customer.

At an overall level, your reader is challenged in one of these three ways:

- **Habits that don't serve them**
  If you can inspire them to change these habits, it will create a continued impact, a better life, and therefore tremendous gratitude and loyalty towards you. They will tell anyone who will listen how your book helped them. Some great examples of authors who do this successfully are Hal Elrod and Mel Robbins (see Chapter 1)

- **Confusion on how to solve the problem**
  A lack of information or information overwhelm can be the root cause of this. Nobody needs information if they know what to look for. What they don't have is a system or recipe or the vocabulary to look up

what they need. Or awareness that there is a solution available to them. Providing a step-by-step framework will be helpful.

- **Confusion on what the problem is**
  The source of this can also be a lack of, wrong, or an overwhelming amount of information. Or thinking there is no solution. Quite often the root cause is underlying beliefs controlling how they think though. Provide credible and original sources. Tell stories that make them question if their limiting belief is always true. Shift their mindset and provide the next steps (they are not necessarily ready for all the steps yet).

Audience research is the key to understanding the nature of the problem your book is solving. Often we tend to describe a problem in terms of what is lacking or what they are looking to achieve. However, we also need to think about the reason they didn't just solve this themselves and how we should present the solution to them: How to change the habit (motivate them to execute the solution), how to implement the best solution (step-by-step), or how to see the problem from a new angle and open up for new solutions.

One of the ways we can know this is - tadaaa….

- by asking them!

I know. It's wild. But you could ;)

Additionally, you could do desk research:

- Google trends
- Answerthepublic.com
- Trending hashtags
- Popular books on Amazon
- Popular blogs, youtube channels, and podcasts

Form a hypothesis about the real nature of their problem. Their fear, and what stopped them from solving it, and then ask open questions to a handful of perfect customers and see if those assumed problems and pains come up in the conversation.

What should your role be in solving their problem? Give information, reveal the truth, put a spotlight on their limiting beliefs, solve the problem entirely, make them believe they can, change a habit, educate them about the steps?

Also listen to which words they use to express their problems, challenges or desires. The reason you should do this is that you should "sell them what they want and give them what they need". These 'want' words are also the words they would type into a search bar and words that perhaps (if not exhausted by competitors) should be part of your title or subtitle. The reader must immediately recognise this book is for him or her.

Now that you have identified and articulated the overall problem and the 4-7 underlying problems, you are ready for the final 2 magical questions:

3. What are **the 3 AHAs** the reader will experience? What are the key takeaways they are so surprised about that they will tell a friend and that it will change how they view the problem? (Your answer to this may move your book from a habit-changing book to a step-by-step book, or from a step-by-step to a mindset-shifting or more visionary book.

4. What are **the questions the reader has** when picking up your book - before reading?

The answers to these questions will further set boundaries for your book but also often provide great hooks, great tweetables, or even a fantastic book title!

They will also help you identify where your customer is at right now so you can meet them in their actual state of mind, offering a solution to the actual questions they have. Phrased in my own words, that's pretty much the lesson we learned from Søren Kierkegaard, the Danish philosopher: If you don't understand people better than they understand themselves, teaching is not only impossible but your effort actually has the sole purpose of you showing off ;)

You could create a great book at any of these intersections. The RIGHT book for <u>you</u> is the one that will attract <u>your</u> PERFECT customer. The profitable customer that you LOVE working with.

With the 4 magical questions answered, you are ready for the next step which is emptying your brain using one of my favourite tools:

The Popcorn Method

1. Have a huge piece of paper cover a huge table

2. Have pens in different colours available and remove the chairs and anything stopping you from moving freely around the table

3. Be alone, shut off your phone, and don't bring your laptop either

4. Draw a circle at the centre and write your topic or anticipated title if you have one (not important)

5. Dedicate the four corners of the paper to the answers to the 4 magical questions, drawing a half-moon and writing them down, one in each corner

6. Hydrate, stare at the paper for a while, and wait for the first pop - your first thought about what should go into the book

7. Write it down somewhere using as few words as possible, preferably no more than three - you'll need the space and just need to be able to remember it and get it down quickly so you can capture the next thought too

8. More and more pops will come, faster and faster - note them as quickly and uninterrupted as you can

9. At some point, pops will come slower - take a short break outside, stargazing for celestial inspiration - do not allow anything to disrupt your flow, aka. don't look at your phone!

10. Start again with a new colour and force yourself to continue until the new colour is even distributed across the paper.

11. Take another break, and start again with a new colour but this time think of only examples, stories and cases you could add, or research you could look into, or whatever you want to be part of your book

It doesn't matter if it becomes a mindmap or not - that can make sense if, for example, your 4-7 underlying problems are put into a step-by-step system. I'd rather call it mind-magic-ing. It's a method designed to allow ideas to pour out of your head and let you capture them randomly on paper.

It's not the goal to focus on structure now. Just randomly jot down all your ideas where you intuitively feel they belong. Seeing the words and colours filling the paper stimulates the right, creative side of your brain and opens the gates to your creative juices, like water flows to and through the Iguazu waterfall; broad, voluminous and seemingly slowly until it reaches the destination - here your paper.

The goal is to EMPTY your head and remember all the gold in there, at this point. If you start judging the content, evaluating where it goes, or spend an unnecessary amount of time thinking of and writing long sentences, you are basically putting up a dam, condemning the goodies so only those at the top will become part of your book. We want all of the goodies on that paper.

Your next step is to create **a book structure.**

Thoroughly complete each of these steps:

1. **How many books** are on the paper? Should you exclude certain parts and save them for a second book?

2. **How many chapters** should the content be contained in? Give them names that help you get a clear vision of the flow of the book - you can sex them up later

3. What are the **core elements** of each chapter? Decide on 3, 4 or 5 bullet points for each chapter. If you feel you need more than 5 bullet points, you probably need to split the chapter in two. If you can't think of at least 3, consider if there is enough to say or it should go into another chapter. This is also a good time to add a page to your fake book proposal with the chapter names and a short description of each chapter. I like to include that page in the book to give the reader an overview of what's to come.

THIS is what I call **front-loading your writing process**. Making all decisions about what goes into your book and not. In this book, the pages Content Clues and the 6 Ps of publishing was pretty much what I had at this point.

But we are far from done yet.

4. Open up Word or Pages or Google Docs and enter the outline you just created. Format with the right headline levels. I use Google Docs because it provides an outline on the left side of my document so I can easily click back and forth (that's why you format the headlines)

5. Transfer all of the information from your huge piece of paper and put it where it belongs. If it doesn't belong, keep it for a LinkedIn post or your next book. Do not worry about too much or too little information right now. Just sort everything into the document in its right spot.

6. Take a break and look at the document with fresh eyes. Work your way through each chapter - one at a time - filling in the gaps and moving bits and pieces around until you have a completely logical flow in each chapter. Pay attention to if you <u>made all decisions</u>, and make those you didn't make.

The detailed outline of your book may end up being 15-20 pages. If you have 4 pages for a 300-page book, I promise you will learn, you did not make all decisions yet. Fight the temptation to start writing! You won't know exactly what to say yet.

Your test of 'good enough' is this: You should be able to present each chapter to an audience of 50 people using your detailed chapter outline as your only preparation. When you can do that, you are ready to write.

Writing better and faster

If there is ONE big idea you take from this book - apart from the fact that you should be self publishing - let it be **front-loading** as described in the previous section. This is what will truly save time and help you create a much better book.

I know you like choices and for this next step, there is more than one way you can go, choosing **your writing strategy.**

For a nonfiction book based on your expertise, I rarely recommend **ghostwriting**. A coach who will co-write with you or an editor yes, but ghostwriting comes with too high of a risk of the book not turning out how you want it to.

The **reporter style** is mostly relevant if you plan to not put an emphasis on your own big idea but rather the ideas of others, ie. through interviewing a bunch of people or having 8 people each write a chapter. That's not recommendable when your goal is to raise your authority. It can be a great book for a lead generation strategy though because you will instantly have ambassadors ready to promote the book, your co-authors.

This leaves us with three options.

If writing **traditionally**, you will start at the top and type it out at whatever speed you can. You could make a 30 or 60-day plan depending on your attempted book length. A rule of thumb is 250 words per page, which means 220 pages = 55,000 words. You'd need to write approximately 1,000 words per day in a 60-day plan, or 2,000 words per day in a 30-day plan.

To help you stay disciplined, you might wanna keep a success "calendar", which can simply be a piece of paper you stick to the wall where you can't avoid seeing it (try the fridge or the coffee maker which seems to be a preferred procrastination destination!). Add horizontal and vertical lines so the paper has 30 squares. As you pursue your goal, you cross out each successful day with a green or red pen, or use stickers to show progression - or lack thereof.

You can make yourself further accountable by posting a photo of it every day on social media and have someone kick your ass if you are not kind enough to yourself to make your most important project your first priority. Or send someone $1k or $10k and tell them, then can keep it if you don't finish by [date]. Pick someone you trust will actually keep the money!

The problem with this plan is, it takes quite a lot of determination to stay disciplined like that for 30 or 60 days - and reality is, in many cases, it ends up being a lot longer. Sh*t happens. Life happens. Business happens. Christmas happens. It's vacation time! The longer the process, the more sh*t happens.

Many of my customers end up choosing a shortcut that allows them to spend more time on making the book better. They choose to **speak** their books (audio record). What you'd do is to prepare yourself for each chapter as if you were about to get on stage in front of hundreds of people and deliver that specific chapter.

Use a voice memo app on your phone to record, and use a mic or headset. Study your notes for the chapter. Physically open the door to the room you want to record in and enter the "stage". Yes, I am serious! Act as if you were actually getting on stage. This will keep you from starting a discussion with yourself half ways through the chapter. You wouldn't do that in front of an actual audience, would you?

Imagine the audience, sitting there eager to listen to your wisdom, and commit to not stopping to think. You know your sh*t. Just deliver the best you possibly can. Save the file with the filename '1'. Then repeat the process for the rest of the chapters. When you are done, use a digital transcription tool or send the whole thing to your someone to deliver a transcript that is more or less cleaned up.

Boom! You have a first full draft in just a couple of days after finishing your detailed outline. You'll likely be close to puking but you can (and should) record the whole damn thing in one day!

I guess, now you see how you can create a first full draft in just a week! The trick is to be SUPER prepared before speaking. Otherwise, you'll just create a lot of rubbish and a lot of editing will be necessary. But that sh*t also happens if you type it out without a proper plan for the content.

Obviously, you can use **AI tools** to write your book. ChatGPT is a popular choice but there are others that are designed to specifically help you as an author.

You might use AI for the entire book. But if that works for you, I would like to challenge you on whether your content does, in fact, include bold, fresh ideas that will make you stand out as an authority.

But oftentimes there will be parts where you can save lots of time using AI. Or you can use AI to improve, make it funnier, write your SEO-infused description etc. Go fancy and be bold in your approach to becoming an author - make it fun and learn something new! - also check the suggested content for validity. AI tools tend to invent sh*t without telling you ;)

For this book, I used AI to plan, to find examples and weird strategies, to find better words, to improve the headlines, and many other things. AI didn't write the book for me but served as my assistant.

So when should you use each strategy?

The **traditional** (you type it out)

- If you love the process of writing
- If you are developing your key concepts in parallel
- If you are good at sticking to a structure and keeping an overview of an extensive amount of material

The **speaker** (you speak it, then transcribe it)

- If you already convey and teach your messages in courses, speeches or similar
- If your concepts and solutions are well-developed and proven in practice
- If you want a shortcut to get published faster

The **AI nerd** (you use AI tools)

- If you have experience prompting for the right tone of voice
- If your book is based on public knowledge (not visionary)
- If you are ok training your AI assistant to understand your novel ideas and concepts

Unfuck writer's block

FRONT LOADING is your best weapon to shield you from the temptation to spaghettify the writing process, just throwing random sh*t in a text document and then spend way too much time waffle ironing the initial draft to give it structure. There is no way you'll rollerblade your way through editing by applying such a process.

And reality is, life tends to bite us in the arse from time to time. Sh*t happens. Life happens. Business happens. Applying writing strategies that stretch over time opens the gates and invites a number of writing enemies to the party. Writing becomes a daunting task. Something else will feel more important (read: less boring). T-Rexing the word count goal for the day while experiencing a rollercoaster of emotions is a recipe for a book not published.

So what can you do, apart from front-loading?

The best tip I can give is that you memoryfoam the writing space to protect you from distractions. Take some time off, escape, get off the grid and mermaid into the ocean of nothingness to work intensively on your book. Be determined not to surface until you have a full first draft. Get into a flow state and work your arse off.

You <u>can</u> get it all done in one take. This happens all the time to the authors I bring to my book-writing camps. They all get far enough to be able to:

1) stay committed to making the book their first priority when they come home because motivation is super high, or 2) hand it over to an editor.

Escaping and dedicating intensive work time will provide:

- Less distractions
- Less life-events happening
- Less business emergencies
- Less re-reading to get back on track (which leads to editing too soon)
- Less doubt about book length and if you have enough content

Pick your writing plan according to your readiness-level and preferred writing strategy to carve out the necessary time in your calendar. Then protect that time like a mama-bear!

Before choosing your plan, be aware of the common pitfalls:

- A longer writing plan is not less risky. More sh*t happens in 60 days than in 30 or 7 days.

- Don't pick the 60-day plan just to not push yourself

- Ask yourself the real reason you need more time

Writing Plans

From idea to a first full draft

7-day writing plan
for nonfiction authors

- If your key concepts are super clear and tested
- Get away for the week
- Writing strategy: speaker

How to spend your time

- ▸ 1 day strategizing
- ▸ 1 day mind-magic-ing and defining chapters
- ▸ 1 day detailing the chapter outline
- ▸ 1 preparing and filling in gaps for each chapter
- ▸ 1 day speaking the whole shebang
- ▸ 1 day transcribing and first rough editing
- ▸ 1 day at the beach to reward yourself

30-day writing plan
for nonfiction authors

- There are primarily two reasons to needing more than 7 days
  - ▸ You are not clear on your message /concepts
  - ▸ You need to do research
- Writing strategy: Traditional or Speaker
- If you are not clear or need research AND want to write traditionally, go with the 60-day plan
- No book under 50.000 words needs more time to first full draft

How to spend your time

▸ Dedicate 1 week to research or concepts - then front load making all decisions
▸ 3 weeks for producing text. Either write X words per day or prep, speak, and transcribe a chapter per day

60-day writing plan
for nonfiction authors

- The slow cooker. Only use this if you plan a longer book and/or your process includes more than writing:

    ▸ Intensive research.
    ▸ Clarity on message or concepts.

- Writing strategy: Traditional or Speaker

How to spend your time

▸ If unclear message or concepts:
    ▸ 30 days to research and frontload
    ▸ 30 days to produce

▸ If you are planning a super long book
    - 1 week frontload
    - 7 weeks to produce text, either writing X words per day, or prep, speak, and transcribe a chapter per day

pre-sell

3

Beyoncé your way to the top

In Chapter 1, I introduced the **3** cornerstones of your marketing plan: **The Audience Growth Plan** (your own audience), the **Network Expansion Plan** (the audiences of others), and the **Amazon Ranking Plan** (audiences who "stumble" upon you). In the planning phase, the most important aspect is WHO to activate and HOW. In this chapter covering phase 3 of the 6 Ps, we are more concerned with WHEN.

Your marketing plan should have **3** phases: Before the launch, the actual launch and after the launch.

	your audience	network audience	ranking
pre-launch			
launch			
post-launch			

There is no one recipe that you can follow. You need to come up with your own plan and kale-smoothie the plan for a healthy balance between effort and expected outcome. Using a simple framework like this table will help increase awareness of WHEN you need to do what and how much you realistically can do when. Again, the more you front-load your marketing and the earlier you start promoting, the more time you have to warm people up.

Bestseller lessons from authors and other artists

There is one thing that almost all successful artists have in common; They have a pre-launch strategy. Months ahead of the release date, they engage and warm up their fans. Entrepreneur Magazine brought an article in June 2022 with 5 marketing strategies to build your brand like Beyoncé[18]:

1. **Share quality content**
    Consistently share content over the longest period of time possible - which is why you wanna start today if you don't already

2. **Zig when everyone else is zagging**
    Beyoncé released her 2022 album as a CD! Find ways to stand out not only in your book content and cover, but in your marketing as well. Do crazy sh*t!

3. **Plan ahead and build anticipating**
    Dah, that's what this chapter is about. Let people know about your book and pre-order your book long before it's actually ready. Engage your audience in the process.

4. **Market holistically**

   Even if you can't be present everywhere, you can be present in other people's audiences - and you can create an impression of being everywhere sharing examples of where you were, like other people's podcasts or magazine interviews.

5. **Incentivise multiple purchases**

   Gary Vaynerchuk applied a strategy giving away NFTs to everyone buying 12 books and giving them to their friends. Beyoncé sells box sets. Many of my authors sell packages to companies that include a number of books and a talk. Or the book comes with a tangible bonus item that's only available for pre-order.

Many other artists apply similar strategies. You can learn a lot from studying what artists like Beyoncé, Taylor Swift or Ed Sheeran, or your favourite artist do.

Successful authors **collect pre-orders,** get on podcasts and do **collaborations** with people in their network to reach as many people as possible. You should do the same.

You don't need to have your book ready before you start collecting pre-orders. What you need is a basic manuscript so your content isn't "moving". You have to know exactly what you are selling. Apart from that, you need the title, the subtitle, the author's name, and a book cover (see Chapter 4). Possibly a super simple landing page. That's it.

Authors who skip this step are missing out. They are missing out on the best proof there is to know your book will be successful: People paying for your book! Also, they will be paying you money that you can direct back into your book promotion.

But most importantly, and this is the main reason we do this, you get to talk about your book months before it comes out which makes it a lot easier to create buzz for your book. Usually, this activity gets you into so many conversations your overall sales in your business will spike for that reason alone! People will check you out once you start talking about your book - partly because many of them would love to be in your shoes! You are a rockstar in their eyes, actually going ahead and writing your book.

The benefits of pre-selling your book are manyfold:

1. Validate title, subtitle and cover (does it convert?)
2. Attract even more people to do launch-collabs
3. Finance your launch ads campaigns
4. Know how many books to print in the first edition
5. Execute all orders at once to spike ranking
6. Get reviews ahead of the launch
7. Create a buzz and prolong the "new book" period
8. Collect leads on your landing page instead of sending everyone to a bookstore
9. ... (I am sure you will discover more)

There are basically two ways you can collect pre-orders; On Amazon (or whatever store you choose) or your website. Each has pros and cons, but quite often what I recommend is that you do your ebook pre-launch on Amazon and your print book on your website (adding a link to the ebook).

How to wisely combine boring sh*t and fun sh*t

Marketing campaigns can be a real drag. But they don't have to be! Before the big pre-launch day arrives (which might not even be that special since you have been talking about your book since the day you started writing it), why not take all that dull and tedious work and sweeten it up with some fun sh*t?

There's no denying it. Launching a book requires lots of work. It involves tasks such as setting up your social media accounts, creating promotional graphics, and building your email list. But it doesn't have to be boring as fuck.

Let's look at some creative ways you can combine the two — fun sh*t and boring sh*t — into an epic pre-launch campaign.

For starters, create a creative and fun giveaway, a one-of-a-kind item related to the theme of your book — like a custom t-shirt with a quote from it. In my case, it could be "Plan sober, write wasted". What ya' think? Should I run with it? Or how about my recent TikTok campaign in which

I record myself putting my book in the bestseller section in real bookstores and encourage other authors to join my #bookshelfie campaign?

You can also create a game to engage your followers. Invite them to solve puzzles or play trivia about the book. This can be done on any social media platform via stories, posts, or live streams. It's an easy way to get people talking and engaged with what you have coming up.

Create a **teaser trailer** or short video preview, or perhaps an author Q&A session with yourself as the guest of honour! Or do LinkedIn audio events, inviting partners from your network to come to talk to you about some of the problems your book deals with.

The one thing all successful authors do is to get booked as a guest on lots and lots of podcasts that serve their audience. This is why I want you to consider WHO you should spend time getting to know while you are still writing your book. Unless you are already a well-known brand, you need either a strong personal connection with the host, a financial benefit (like a share of revenues from the book and/or a course that complements the book), or a topic that is truly unique and relevant to the audience. Preferably all of those. Or you'll have to aim a little lower in terms of who you are targeting. That said, all podcast hosts are looking for new guests and it's usually not that difficult to get invitations. There are even services out there that will help you with that.

Book pre-launch campaigns don't have to be all tedious work — there's plenty of room for fun sh*t too! By combining both, you can create an exciting and engaging campaign that will help you build a larger audience and get readers excited about your book before it's even released. The sky is the limit and you can do whatever the hell you want. That's the fun part of being a self published indie author!

Be clear on when you are making the shift from creating buzz to sales conversion. Up until you start collecting pre-orders (asking people to buy, expecting a later delivery date), your main focus will be collecting email subscribers interested in your book and keeping those leads hot as hell. Have a plan for how you'll fire them up while waiting for your book.

Here are some of the things to include in your pre-launch plan:

- Get your cover ready as soon as you are sure about the title (make sure you did your keyword research to include in the title and/or subtitle)
- Pre-order form on your website
- Pre-order ebook on Amazon (you can set that up 12 months before - 3 months is recommended)
- Create a profile on Amazon Author Central
- Change your bios on social media
- Change your email signature
- Ask for reviews
- Create a book trailer

- Have a posting plan (upload chapters to an AI tool to speed up the process)
- Plan for Collabs (how many, who, what do you offer to the collab partner and/or the audience?)

Maintaining 100% ownership

Now before you share anything about your title, subtitle, cover, or key concepts, a quick reminder about ownership and copyrights.

Copyrights are super important but the significance is often overlooked. First of all, copyrights can be traded. This means that you'll want to keep all rights yourself, which is the main reason you want to be self publishing.

From a practical perspective, you obtain copyrights to your work (book or other formats) the second you create them. Adding a copyright page (or with a fancy word, a colophon) at the beginning of your book will be the declaration of your copyrights - and also guidance to anyone who considers using something from your book, adding it to their own content, articles or teaching sessions.

Making your work publicly available is a great way to protect your copyright. That is also a great reason to hurry up and get your expert model published in your name before anyone runs with your idea, hopefully without realising that's not how it works.

So copyright protection is automatically granted to your book, as long as your book is an original work. As stated on the US Copyright Office's site: "Your work is under copyright protection the moment it is created and fixed in a tangible form that it is perceptible either directly or with the aid of a machine or device." Essentially, once you've written your book, you don't have to actively apply for copyright protection. It's already there.

I recommend that writers outside of the US investigate the particular country's copyright protection laws. You may be required to apply for the protection. In most countries, to the best of my knowledge, no registration is required, but it is easier to document the ownership if registered. In the US, dealing with any legal matters that may occur will be much easier if you registered your copyrights with the proper authorities.

Likewise, you don't want to be violating any copyrights held by others. The best way to use their content is to have permission to do so. Always name them and reference their work - and read the copyright page in their books. Sometimes you'll need to research if anyone published something similar before and credit them. Using some of the plagiarism tools out there makes the process a lot easier.

polish

4

Perfecting your masterpiece

The bad news is that even though you are off to a great start and spent 20% of your time getting 80% done, you still have a lot of work to do. The good news is you are now at a level where you can hire people to help you finish your book. The content is no longer stuck in your brain.

Polishing your book is about:

1. Completing your manuscript

   - Ninja-edit the body of the manuscript
   - Add the missing pages (I'll give you a list)
   - Include lead magnets
   - Re-edit the whole shebang for readability
   - Proofreading (shouldn't be you doing that)
   - Secure even distribution of illustrations
   - Add ISBNs
   - Include guiding comments for the designer

2. Making decisions about how to publish

   - Understand the terms of each platform
   - Determine the formats to offer
   - Are physical bookstores important?
   - Is there a maximum length for your book?
   - Will you need/want to keep it black/white?

3. Designing the book

- Create a selling book cover (for each format)
- Layout all of the pages inside your book
- Format for chosen formats (how meta is that?)

Taking your manuscript to the highest level

Writing and editing a book are two different things. Writing is about getting the content out of your head and onto the page in a structured way. Perhaps you'll discover that you firework-exploded the content when speaking it, getting off track a million times. Well, it's still out of your head. Editing focuses on refining and improving an already-existing manuscript. It does not only involve looking for typos and errors in grammar or punctuation (that's proofreading).

During the first round of editing, there is a significant focus on structural problems such as poor transitions between paragraphs, and aspects of the narrative that need to be strengthened. This is when we are jukeboxing the perfect words all night long to find the perfect way to enhance learning, entertain, and seek to convert readers to potential customers by showing our personality even more. Sunshine-and-rainbow the manuscript with colourful prose if that's our style. Fact-base and set of the nerd alert if that's our style.

So do you need an editor?

Maybe. No. And yes.

There are two types of editing:

1. Content editing (also called developmental editing)

    - Is the flow good?
    - Writing style, personality
    - Gets your point across
    - Testing your content (promise fulfilled?)
    - Likely to attract ideal clients?
    - Are there repetitions?
    - Are there parts where things are explained in an overly complicated manner?
    - Are parts of the content obsolete?

2. Copy editing, extended proofreading (always needed)

    - Grammar is good
    - Word choices
    - Typos
    - Redundancies
    - Inconsistencies
    - Links

Some of these things can be super hard, if not impossible, to do yourself. Your head is too far up where the light doesn't shine to be able to see your mistakes and room for improvement clearly. There is a risk you'll miss something but even more so, a risk that you spend forever not finishing your book because uncertainty about the content creeps in.

You can do a self-evaluation of your writing on a scale from 1 to 10. How good is your writing? Are you writing in your native language? Could your text benefit from enhanced richness and variation? Is it stiff and boring or fun and vibrant? How sure are you about the flow, consistency and readability of your book?

You should always have a proofreader. If you feel super confident about your content, you might just ask the proofreader to pay special attention to a few other things too and skip the editor and self-edit it.

If you want to hire an editor or co-writing book coach, you can easily find one at Upwork or a similar 3rd party platform. Find someone with experience and knowledge about your topic.

Either way, **always self-edit** first. Make the content as good as you possibly can yourself, before handing it over. Unless you work with a co-writing book coach. Someone who really gets your business and the strategy your book is a part of.

Once you are done, here are a few more things to consider:

- **Up the first 10%**
  As mentioned previously, some bookstores offer a 10% sample preview to potential buyers. Make sure that the first 10% of your content sells the book. The

first 10% is real estate you don't want to blah blah away with a story about how you have learned what's in the book. Nobody cares and you will sound like you are not an expert. And by the way, bookstores also get a preview of your book. Depending on how you publish there may be an option to include more information to help them select the best books for their store.

- **Read your book aloud**

  Do not make the mistake of not reading your own book aloud before finishing the script. Reading aloud will eliminate two problems. Firstly, what sounds weird reading it aloud or is difficult to say without taking breaths or twisting your tongue, will also be unappealing to your reader. Secondly, it will be a mess when you record your audiobook! Read aloud and mark unclear sections and pay special attention to the text around illustrations. Make the book readable without the illustration. When you are done reading, make the necessary adjustments.

- **Add must-have and could-have pages**

  One of the tricks I often use to make the writer feel like an author once we start editing is adding the pages that will make the document feel like a book and not an incredibly long blog post that no one will read. There is nothing more discouraging than a never-ending wall of text. Add the pages that will separate the parts. Add page numbers. Format headlines to the right level (heading 1, 2, 3). And add the must-have pages and could have pages: Copyright page, about the author page (includes a short bio, author image, contact information, social links, and website), acknowledgements, foreword (written by someone cool your audience knows with a purpose to sell the book), preface (why you are qualified to write the book).

- **Revisit the introduction**

  The introduction differs from the foreword and preface and should be part of the actual writing process, not something you add later. In its first version, it should be closely related to the fake book proposal you created in Chapter 1. But it is often also the last thing I rewrite because I quite often realise important points while editing the manuscript. I recommend you revisit it and tighten it up and reconsider if there is an even stronger hook for your book.

- **Add a lead magnet**

  The purpose of your book is to open up more business opportunities. What makes sense to add to your book in terms of capturing leads will depend on your strategy. If you are looking to turn readers into customers for your backend product, finding a way to incentivise them to subscribe to your email list should be a key priority. Identify where you might have gone one step deeper and create a lead magnet to help the reader get results quicker, with less effort, or with a better result. Then add the lead magnet URL on the copyright page, directly in the text or as a separate page. If you published other books, showing the cover of those at the end is a great way to deepen the relationship with the reader. Always make it easy for the reader to take the next logical step on their journey with you - but don't sound like a goddamn dishwasher commercial either. Make it about the reader, not about you.

- **Add endorsement pages (book blurbs)**
A study by BookBub found that a quote from a well-known author boosted the click-through rate by 22%. If you know a big shot in your niche, give it a go. But let's face it, most new authors don't have access to that. Try and build relationships with relevant industry professionals or authors writing on similar topics or to similar audiences, starting long before you ask for their help. Be helpful to them first. There are several ways to use endorsements. Adding a couple of pages with blurbs can be very powerful. You might even want to put the most potent one on your book cover (someone your reader knows or who has a title that instantly signals authority). Quotes from less well-known authors can be placed in your Author Central Editorial Review section or be included in the metadata if your platform allows it.

Book cover fuckups
and what to do instead

The list of how you can possibly fuckup a book cover is endless. For this reason, my very first point has to be that you work with a professional. But you're smart, and you have no interest in messing around trying to learn how to do stuff like that. But you still need to be able to ask for the right thing and evaluate the suggestions you receive.

Fuckup #1 - Genre and subject miscommunication

You have a split second to capture attention and let your perfect reader understand this is relevant to them. As an example, don't choose a big portrait of yourself on the front cover if you are not already a known face to your audience. They might think it's a memoir. The visuals and the title must support each other and make it obvious what the book is about at the overall level.

As a side note, I only recommend using your own face on the cover if there is a point in stressing you are DIFFERENT from others in your industry. One of my favourite authors is a super cool lady who is rocking the security sector which is dominated by men. Her face blended into an image of a large city gone dark has worked really well and captures the attention of readers. Make sure there is a strategic reason and not a vanity reason behind it. If you wanna check out the book, her name is Susanne Diemer and the title is 'Your Urban Crisis Survival Planner'.

Fuckup #2 - Wrong branding and wrong targeting

The cover should attract and call out your ideal customer. I know you wanna love your book but a design that doesn't fit your brand or what the customer can expect from you might convert in terms of book sales but it won't convert readers to customers. Often there is an overlap between your taste and theirs but sometimes there is not. Sometimes what seems perfect just won't stand out in the market. Sometimes it doesn't match the experience the - then potential customer - gets on your website. Your book is a masterpiece in and of itself - but the higher value comes from making smart book funnel decisions and creating a coherent experience attracting people to your business that you will love working with.

Fuckup #3 - Bland design, wrong fonts or font size

Font type, font size, font colour, image or illustration all matter in terms of readability. You also can't have too many elements competing for attention. A book cover should draw readers in with a few well-placed elements that are easy to read and understand. If online sales are a significant goal for you, consider the fact that people will see your book cover in 2x1" as they scroll past rows of tiny book covers. Check your categories and make sure it stands out and that the title can be read 2 feet from your computer screen.

Fuckup #4 - Using stock photos

With or without permission - it's a horrible idea unless you are the ONLY person owning that image. If you use a designer you don't know already, ask for documentation that you can legally use the image. Or have them create something that is a mix of multiple images so it is a new original. Or create one in Midjourney or another AI tool … or avoid using images altogether. Many nonfiction books don't have a front cover image. Often some graphical designs look and work better.

Fuckup #5 - Not using the real estate of the back cover
The back cover should be used to sell books. Too often I see authors talking about solutions or sharing their stories instead of creating curiosity with the back cover text. Have a strong hook so the potential reader immediately understands why they should buy this book. Remind them of their pain points. Amplify the pain a little. Then give hope about a solution without giving one. Add a few sentences that reveal why you are the right person to help. Perhaps a few cool people endorsing the book.

Bestselling book formats

A thing that all the bestsellers have in common is attention to detail. Even if you've got amazing content, if the formatting is off, it will be hard for readers to take your work seriously. If you hire a great editorial designer to do your layout you can almost just skip ahead to the next section in this book. You'll need to give them some input though so here is what characterises bestselling books.

First off, the **page size** is incredibly important. In general, nonfiction books have a larger page size than fiction books. It can also be too big though and feel like an elementary school book - and that's not good! Which size suits your content depends on how many pages your book is (in that size), how your book is illustrated (or not), who your target audience is, and so many other factors. Get a few sample pages from your designer that includes all vital elements that are part of your design concept and print it out in ACTUAL SIZE - not FIT TO PAGE to get a feeling of what it will look like.

A big book might feel impressive. But it's also not handy to bring and read on the go. It can seem overwhelming to read, impossible to read one hand only at the beach, or your reader just doesn't want that much depth on the subject at this point. A smaller, pocket-size book could be your best option! For my last book, I was inspired by the book 'Tribes' by Seth Godin, one of the most successful authors in the marketing space. Before starting to write, I made it my goal that the book should be about 150 pages long and in a close-to-pocket-size format. Why? Because that's enough to cover the subject to the level the reader of that book is ready to invest time to.

Font choice is another essential aspect of formatting. Typography can be a tricky thing to get right, so spend some time researching other books. Find 5 you like and send them to your designer. Don't try to be an expert yourself. A good designer knows what works. What you need to know though is that changing a font can add or subtract 20-30 pages from your book. So keep an eye on the total book length before you approve the design concept! Also make up your own mind, if you want a serif or sans serif font.

For **line spacing**, it depends on the type of book you are writing. Should you know this stuff? Not really. However, changing the setting on the document you write your manuscript in will give an idea of how many pages your book will end up having. Set the page size, margins and line spacing.

I don't want to go too much into detail and I am pretty sure you are getting bored already. You are not gonna be a goddamn designer. Just hire someone, will ya?

But hire a great one with a portfolio that includes books in the style you are looking for and ask for:

- Fixed price per page
- Unlimited revisions
- Source files included

Now, let's circle back to **which book formats should you offer?**

I know you want to have print books. Got it.

Here are a few things to consider:

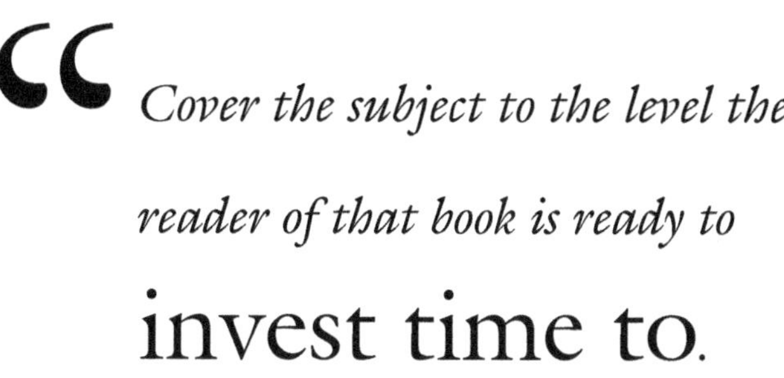

Cover the subject to the level the reader of that book is ready to **invest time to.**

- A big part of retail book sales are hardcover so yes, you should have that if you want retailers to pick up your book. If you are primarily using your book as a business card to sell B2B, a hardcover might also be your best option.

- If you wanna use your book as a lead generator and set your price lower, the paperback is a lot less expensive, printing and shipping alike. And lots of people prefer paperbacks for their lower weight, flexible cover and usually lower price.

- If you publish your book using print-on-demand (Chapter 5), there really is no reason not to have both.

My recommendation: Have both and use them for different purposes. Why the hell should you underserve the diverse needs within your target segment when you can serve them all with little effort? Reading preferences are real and not providing the preferred format might prevent your next best client from getting your book.

But what about digital formats? Let's start with the easiest to create, the ebook format.

- 32% of Americans claim they only read print books
- 33% say they read both print books and e-books
- 9% say they only read e-books

But do people in your audience read ebooks? Here are some indicators of who will prefer an ebook[19]:

- Younger (42% if under 30y, 28-32% if 30-65y)
- Black or white (Hispanic much lower)
- College degree
- Higher income
- Urban

In 2020, 22.7% of people in the US and 20% of people in the UK purchased an ebook.

- Doesn't weigh anything in a suitcase or purse
- You can read on all devices
- You can change the font or font size
- You can read at night (change background colour)

And it's less expensive. That's not important because your reader can then afford it. If they can't afford a book then they can't afford you. They are not relevant as a lead. Yet, the lower price point is important. People buy ebooks first to see if they like the book - then buy a print format. Or they buy both. Again, you are missing out on part of your potential target segment if you don't offer an ebook. Don't worry about the less impressive format. Ebook readers expect that.

No matter your distribution choices, your ebook should be available on Amazon, which practically owns the e-reader market:

- 72% Amazon Kindle
- 10% Barnes & Noble Nook
- 18% Other apps

You need to convert your book into an ebook. Find someone on Upwork, there is no reason to bother learning how to do that. It's quite inexpensive. Self publishing platforms offer some functionality to do it yourself. I find the solutions inadequate. Find a pro.

What about audio?

Well, again, you are missing out on some people in your target segment if you don't offer an audiobook. Here are some additional numbers[20] to convince you to go through the hassle of creating an audio version of your book:

- Audio accounted for 3.8% of global book revenue in 2022 and is projected to rise to 4.73% in 2023 and 21.39% in 2030
- In the US, 9% of all book sales in 2022 was audio
- Audiobook revenue exceeded ebook revenue in 2019
- Over 74,000 audiobooks published in the US in 2022

Want some indicators your target audience listens?

Here are the early adopters, those who listen more frequently:

- Younger
- Black
- Women

"*Audiobooks are projected to account for more than* 20% of global book revenue *in 2030.*

But bear in mind that a quarter of all Americans listened to an audiobook in 2021 and 45% by 2022 listened to at least one in their life. In any target segment, you'll be losing out if you don't offer an audio format.

There used to be a but. It used to be quite expensive to produce an audiobook. Here is why production cost is no longer an excuse:

- People wanna hear the author's voice in a nonfiction book - get a Yeti or other podcast mic and record it in your closet. A perfect environment for audio recording!
- Import to Descript, remove 'eehms' and 'uhms' with the 'remove filler words' feature designed to do just that, edit the text. Yes, the text! - not audio. It will transcribe it so you can easily see where you repeated yourself and edit directly in the text, and as you do so, it will remove those same passages from the audio. Super smart! Turn on 'studio quality', and export with the right settings.
- Send the files to an audio editor to prep the files to comply with platform requirements, and booom! You are ready to publish your audiobook. And the quality will be great too!

So, yes! You should also publish in audiobook format.

NFWhat?!?

NFT means Non-Fungible Token. Not gonna explain that in this book, since I wrote a whole damn book about it last year. It's called 'NextGen Author' and is a visionary book about where book publishing is heading. The newest trends and the technologies and behaviours driving them. You should read it! ;)

I do want to mention here that NFT publishing is becoming a thing - slowly but surely are services appearing that will help authors:

- Document ownership
- Get paid fairly on first sale AND repeat sale
- Own customer data
- Deliver additional value over time to book owners
- Develop deeper author-reader relationship
- Crowdfound their books

Go to Amazon, get the book, give me a review ;)

Pre-publication decisions

There are a few decisions that might seem related to the publishing step but that should be made before designing the book. You need to know where you are going to publish and what the requirements are on that particular platform (or printer).

- Chapter 5 will dive deeper into your choice of platform. If you choose print-on-demand publishing, you need to be aware of the risk of your book becoming too expensive. The two factors to keep that under control are the book-length (keep it under 250 designed book pages), and the use of colour. The more coloured pages, the more expensive. You can easily have a beautiful design and avoid colours altogether (except for the cover but that doesn't influence print costs).

- The actual measurements of the book are called the trim size. Your designer needs to know what size to design your book for. When you publish via a self publishing platform, there are a number of trim sizes available to you. Make sure your preferred size is available in both hardback and paperback. Most if not all self publishing platforms will offer expanded distribution, meaning they will make it available to 3rd party bookstores. Check that your selected trim size is eligible for expanded distribution.

- Note that ebooks are not the PDFs you are offered as part of marketing funnels. An ebook is an HTML book offering features to the reader like being able to change the font, font size, background colour, and page size (reading on a smartphone, iPad, laptop, pc or even TV). A complicated design will be rather messed up when it's converted to ebook format.

Keeping it simpler will make your ebook look a lot better. As mentioned, a significant part of almost any audience prefers the ebook format. Deselecting the ebook format for design reasons also means eliminating the opportunity to use Amazon to pre-sell your book.

- If you plan for an audiobook version, your cover design should take that into consideration. An audiobook cover is usually square.

publish

5

Print, Pixel & PoD Potpourri

This might be the most important chapter of the entire book. Honestly, there is only one way to say it: The book publishing industry is a little fucked up. So much is based on ancient needs (of the power lords) and there is little innovation happening, even with the introduction of print-on-demand which has, in all fairness, allowed indie publishers to reach far more readers than before.

Yeah, I know, new book formats have also been introduced and online bookstores and their algorithms have definitely influenced the industry. But many of the most important aspects that directly affect author income and control have not changed at all - and things are rarely in the author's favour.

This chapter aims to educate you about how publishing actually works. All you need to know is here - but if you wanna go deeper, and know how the industry is likely to undergo a disruption sooner or later, you really should go pick up a copy of NextGen Author, my previous book that I just mentioned. Meanwhile, our focus is to optimise for your **long-term success** as an author.

Print distribution vs. print-on-demand

Traditional publishers forecast and analyse market demand, make a plan for which books to serve the market with, find authors to write for those sweet spots, and purchase the rights for books.

Their profitability depends on:

- **Large volume printing** to get print costs down - or overflood the market for the book to be "everywhere". However, if these books end up being destroyed or sold at a fraction of the price to ie. BookOutlet to get rid of them, the authors have no interest in large volume printing. Apart from the obvious environmental impact that overproducing brings.

- **Addressing mass market needs** and publishing fewer books that sell more to keep development costs down. It's not in your best interest because your goal is to obtain authority in a particular niche, not to compete with well-established personal brands with huge marketing budgets, and book funnels that are so efficient they can give their books away for free.

- **Owning and selling rights** to the book, ie. for international markets, some of the formats, etc. When they buy rights to your book they also obtain creative rights and the right to change the book however they like, to take it off the market, or refuse to publish it if you don't comply with their demands.

I promise I won't ramble on about traditional publishing but before we move on, there are a couple of things more you need to know:

- A traditional publisher **will do little marketing** for you unless you are such a big name you wouldn't need this book. In fact, their first question might be how many books <u>you</u> can promise to sell (asking you to document followers, email subscribers, usual conversion rates etc.) It is common that only a fraction of the publisher's marketing resources go to new authors. The overwhelming majority goes to their top-performing authors. In short, you do the marketing. Not them.

- Another reason why many dream of a publishing deal is a lack of **knowledge**. On how to write a book, how to get books into bookstores, how to choose the right title, the list of things that seem unfamiliar is endless. I know that's not you. You are a go-getter and you know you can easily find someone to help you - without giving away the rights to your book.

- Finally, some believe the publisher's brand on the spine will somehow magically sell more books because people will trust it's a quality book. Also not you. You can't even remember when you last checked for that when you bought a book. There used to be some truth in it though. But that's because early self publishing books looked like crap. Today, they come in the same high quality - if you make the right choices.

- Publishing traditionally **takes a lot longer** - and you'll be waiting for your money even longer. There are more people involved, the publisher took a risk on your book and they don't actually publish that many books so they need to make sure it will hit the market hard. They invest resources and the books they pick must be home runs.

You will do the marketing. You will pay through your royalties. And you will NOT have your book in the market for the next 18-24 months, attracting customers and business opportunities to your business. You will need to be patient and learn how to operate in the world of traditional publishing, not being able to make your own decisions.

All that said, I think it's obvious, my recommendation to entrepreneurs and thought leaders is to self publish.

But how?

I know you will love you have options so here they are:

- Publish in the exact same way as the traditional publisher; **print books and distribute them** using the exact same system they do for storage, fulfilment, and for making them available for bookstores to select for their catalogue.

- Use a **print-on-demand** solution like KDP (an Amazon company) or Ingramspark (an Ingram company), both of which will let you keep all rights to your book.

The first option may be the most interesting one to you if you expect to sell a lot of books, or if you plan to sell most of the books directly to your B2B customers or as a part of a public speaking package you offer. The advantage is you get to keep more of the profits from books and don't pay royalties to anyone.

There are a few downsides too, however. You'll need to estimate and print the optimal amount of books. And you'll need to keep an eye on when stock is running out and order a new print in time. And if you are not using a fulfilment centre, you'll be the one (or someone employed by you) to pack and ship the books.

Print-on-demand implies uploading the print-ready file (that you would otherwise send to a printer) to a PoD platform. When you publish your book, it will automatically be included in the platform's own catalogue (if it has a bookstore) and made available to other bookstores too (that's what's called expanded distribution). You'll quickly see your book being available in online bookstores since they really have no risk when including your book title in their catalogue. It's all hands-off; a book details page is created automatically for your book, and when a customer buys your book, an order will be sent through the system to your PoD platform which will then print a book and send it to the customer. The PoD platform will also handle all parts of the money flow, including paying royalties to you.

There are downsides to PoD too. Because one book is printed at a time, the cost of each book is higher than when printed in bulk. Sometimes a lot higher. In Chapter 4, I mentioned you'll need to keep your page count and use of colours at a reasonable level (or not use colour at all inside the book). If your print cost is too high, you are forced to set your sales price too high - and you won't make a profit at all. I also already mentioned limitations in terms of trim sizes. There will be a selection to choose from but some platforms offer more variety than others. Ingramspark has a lot more options and also offers more variety on paper quality, flaps on the cover, jacket for the hardcover etc. It is often also a little more expensive.

These things change over time so my intention is not to go into too much detail here or recommend a specific platform over another but to give you enough information for you to know that you need to look this up before choosing your platform and your design. There are a number of other factors that also might be important to you, like whether you want to be able to offer physical bookstores a return policy (which is pretty much a requirement), when and how royalty payout happens, differences in marketing options, whether you can use your own ISBN or they will give you one, which markets you can reach with their service, etc.

You don't need to establish a separate company to self publish. You only need to decide on an IMPRINT name which is what you would often consider the publishing company name. My print name is Publishing Rebel. It could also be my own name, my legal company name, or the name of the PoD platform. Establishing a new legal entity mostly makes sense from a legal point of view, if you want to protect your business from any risk related to the book, or if you want to protect the rights to your book in case your business goes south.

There is a third and fourth option. The third is combining the two self publishing methods. Even if you want to print the majority of your books yourself, you can upload them to print-on-demand too, for example, if you primarily sell on your website or direct sales B2B but also want somewhere to send an individual or to be present in major bookstores if someone looks you up online.

The fourth is actually somewhat hilarious.

Hybrid publishing is a combination of traditional and self publishing. So there are two options here;

- The hybrid publisher obtains rights to your book, in which case the hybrid part really is just more transparent in the fact that you PAY for them to publish it. They are a traditional publisher then.

- Or they don't obtain rights, in which case, there is no reason to call it a publisher at all. My services fall in the latter category - but I call myself a book coach and not a publisher.

To be clear:

You. Don't. Want. A. Publisher.

You want:

Control. Ownership. Help to publish better and faster.

Learn how we help experts
become published authorities

The 3 digital formats (ebook, audio, NFT)

In the section about bestselling book formats, I shared information about which formats to publish, including the digital formats. I want to take the opportunity to write the shortest (maybe ;) chapter ever on WHERE to publish those formats.

Here is what you need to know:

- There are many ways to get your ebook published. The most popular option is to use KDP, which is Amazon's own platform. But there are other options.

- Your audiobook depends on where you reside. As a Danish resident, I can't publish directly via ACX which is also an Amazon company. Findaway Voices or Authors Republic are two great options for wider distribution (also for non-US/UK residents). There are lots of services popping up - read the terms!

- NFT publishing services are still quite limited. I used Readl.io for my previous book 'NextGen Author'. Super easy process. I will be testing out more services as they are mature enough for what I want. Get the book if you wanna learn more about this - NFTs are the main topic.

The art of selling with metadata

Unless you are planning to only sell your books through direct channels, you must understand how retail works. Whether you are looking to sell in physical bookstores or online, metadata is your key to success. Physical bookstores will use them to find the books they will allow to take up shelf space (aka books with the quickest turnaround). For online bookstores, you must learn how to salsa with algorithms, making them work with you and show your bootie off (book!, sorry about that) to the right people (aka your favourite client).

There are few good reasons not to care about your online presence. In fact, I can't think of a reason not to optimise it. First of all, even if you don't care about online sales at all, people will expect to find an authority's books in major book outlets. Secondly, you are tapping into an ecosystem of buyers with their credit cards ready to buy.

- Amazon has 2.72 billion unique monthly visitors (2023)
- 89% of US consumers are more likely to buy products from Amazon than from any other e-commerce site
- Amazon is responsible for over 50% of sales from the Big Five publishers and controls 50%-80% of the book distribution in the US[21]

"You must learn how to salsa with algorithms. The key to your success is metadata.

- According to Bowker records, Amazon's market share of self-published print books in the US increased from 6% in 2007 to 92% as of 2018.[22]

It's really a no-brainer that your ebook and prints should be on Amazon (and your audio since you now know it's not a huge investment and a big chunk of your target group prefer listening over reading) - and of course your books should also be available in all other major bookstores.

So how do you ask the algorithm for a dance?

Well, flirting isn't gonna do the trick for you. You need to be direct and take the initiative. Introduce yourself.

The algorithm excels at optimising store revenue. It works relentlessly to figure out how to show the right product to the right customer, producing the perfect customer experience in which the customer needs to spend the least amount of time finding exactly what they were looking for.

When your book is registered in the book catalogue, the algorithm will look for information in the metadata to learn what your book is about and who it's for. Obviously, your metadata must **accurately describe** your book, or the algorithm will quickly learn that even though people might look at your book page they are not buying or they give poor reviews later on because the book was not what they expected.

But even with accurate metadata, your book will still need to compete with other books, also accurately described with the same keywords and categories, and show your book at the top of the search results page.

This means:

- You must find keywords that accurately describe your book and that enough people are actually typing into the search bar (there are tools to know this). Some of these will be too competitive, meaning you are up against authors who sell a lot of books using those same keywords. Pick **non-competitive** ones for your book to rise to the surface. Rather have a large portion of a smaller search volume than never reach the surface in a bigger pool. The same goes for categories.

- You must **glue** your selected keywords to your book, not just add them as information about your book (metadata). Algorithm developers know authors will strategically select non-competitive keywords, sometimes at the expense of the customer experience if the keywords aren't accurate for what the book is about. Yeah, you're right. The algorithm will eventually figure out if the book doesn't sell or people are not happy with it, and it will sink to a lower ranking, but meanwhile, the experience isn't great. Therefore, the algorithm is designed to look for signs that the book is, in fact, relevant to the specific search. When you are including your keywords in your book description, in your subtitle, and even in your book title, the algorithm is more quickly able to learn if your data are consistent with the product you are selling. This is also why your evaluation of keyword relevance should include researching whether competing books are using those keywords in the title, subtitle and description.

- As mentioned, the algorithm will also look at **sales data** (did your book details page convert into a sale), **customer satisfaction** (is your book getting positive reviews, and where **traffic** is coming from (preferably, you'll have both organic traffic from search and external traffic sending buyers to their store). This is why your book details page is super important and why you should spend time optimising it.

There is kind of a dilemma here. You want to show the algorithm that everybody loves your book. But you also want to attract the exact right buyers for your business. This is why I encourage you to not optimise your keywords for any buyer but to find keywords that only your favourite customer would type into the search bar. Maybe a phrase only they know about. A specific language style they would use. Letting your cover scream loud and call upon the attention of exactly those people. Your perfect client will want to not spend time looking at books less relevant than yours. Help them find your book quickly.

As a final remark, consider how to capture leads from your book (possibly even from the preview only, adding your free offer in the first 10% of your book). Make additional resources available on your website. Make an offer that will suck your favourite customer into your book funnel.

- Offering a no-brainer small product (at a rather low price) can finance a powerful ads campaign that will kickstart your Amazon ranking and give you loads of visibility.

- It will also give you subscribers for your email list and qualified leads for your more profitable products or services (they already showed both interest and commitment to buying that first product and clearly have the problem you can help solve).

- And the no-brainer product can be used as a great incentive for partners to promote your book for you.

The 99% cases where launch-day doesn't matter

Far too much emphasis is put on launch-day. I won't go into the specifics of the perfect launch day; there are enough books about that already. What I'd rather talk about is the many cases where the actual launch day doesn't really matter.

Launch day is technically the day your book becomes available for purchase. Traditionally, that's the day you will host your book reception, pop the bubbles, and celebrate! You made it to the finish line.

And that's the exact reason why I am not a fan of putting too much emphasis on launch day. Sure there are great strategies to send loads of people from your email list to the bookstore and buy your book and hit top ranking on the first day (in fact, that's not hard at all if you have a large email list or a massive advertising budget). And it is a reality that you need to sell almost all of your books in the first week if you want to hit any of the major bestseller lists (but you will drop off the list if you can't sustain it).

What you are looking for is long-term success with your book.

Here is what I think:

- Launch day is far less important than your pre-launch campaigns. And when you do your pre-order campaign right, pre-orders will all be delivered on launch day, spiking your ranking anyway. So focus on pre-orders! This will give you a lot more time to figure out what works, ie. by testing different kinds of ads.

- Launch day is not the finish line. It's the end of the prep phase for the marketing marathon to come. Up until this point, everything was about creating and dressing your new asset right. Your book will serve you for many years to come and your marketing plan reflects that and includes both pre-launch campaigns,

"Launch day *is not the finish line. It's the end of the prep phase for the* marketing marathon *to come.*

launch, first 90 days, and a long-term plan to keep generating traffic to your page.

- Book receptions are expensive! Imagine putting that money into ads instead to reach a lot more people. There are endless ways to celebrate and create hype about the book using strategies that are both more fun and more effective than serving snacks and drinks to 50 people hoping they will all write a review afterwards. If you wanna party, by all means, do so. But as a marketing tool, the launch party is insignificant unless you more creatively engage the right people (ie. hosting a live virtual launch party with guests who are bringing their audiences). Frankly, if your book reception is a key element in your marketing plan (which it often is!), you are not ambitious enough. Your book's success will be limited and you are leaving money on the table. Make your party grand and mighty - but be smart about it.

- That said, if your online sales are important to you, you should spend time carefully planning your traffic to your book details page, not only for pre-launch and launch day (which is important after all) but for the long haul too.

promote

6

Marketing Bonanza

Despite our intentions, there is a real risk of pancaking on the couch after the extreme burst of creativity, perseverance and nervousness any first-time author experiences. Even if you moonwalked through the writing process, publishing can very much feel like the finish line. It's not. Everything up to here was just preparation.

Information about what works, in general, is super blurry and often of little value to your specific situation. You need to figure out what works for you, given the opportunities you have (or can create!), and the amount of resources you have available and are willing to invest, in terms of money and time.

Getting eyeballs on your book doesn't happen without effort. My suggestion is you make it a mix of classic, scalable, and outsourceable (tedious as they are!) strategies, and fun, maybe quarterly, creative and very uncommon campaigns that fall into the categories of 'shareable', 'engaging', and 'energy creating' campaigns, you will truly enjoy carrying out.

The real difference between sprint and marathon

Apart from the obvious timespan and perseverance differences, the real difference between a long-term and short-term book marketing plan comes down to which **assets** are created in the process. An advertising campaign can run for either a short or a long time - but rarely produces any long-term assets. Once the campaign stops (once you stop sending out emails, once you stop posting on social media, once you stop…), the traffic will stop.

The key component for a long-term book marketing strategy is that you create assets that will serve you over time so that your effort will have an accumulative impact on your business over time:

- **Discoverable content** that will show up in search. This includes podcast episodes, blog posts, YouTube videos, Pinterest boards, short-form videos, LinkedIn articles, articles in industry-relevant media, etc.

- **Strategic peer-to-peer friendships** to cross-promote, co-create campaigns, refer clients to and get referrals from, to interview on your podcast, to do audio events with on LinkedIn, the be recommended by for speaking gigs, to learn and grow with.

The latter is often missing from the marketing plans that authors present to me - often because it can feel like taking advantage of or not consistent with how we view friendship. We don't usually build friendships because we need something from them. We build them for mutual benefit.

New flash! That's exactly why I call them strategic friendships and not just partners or relationships. You don't need a goddamn contract or to dress up for tough negotiations. You need to be a friend first. Cheer each other on. Be helpful. Find ways to both benefit from doing something great together. And this is why I encouraged you to start building more of those relationships back in Chapter 1. You need a **Network Expansion Plan** and to prioritise time to find, build, and nurture those relationships long before you need their help.

Most will agree that creating discoverable content is a great idea - but when time is a scarce resource, tasks with an immediate benefit often win. I had a hard time finding accurate data but the word on the street is that 90% of podcasts won't get past 3 episodes. And of those that do get past 3 episodes, 90% won't get past 20 episodes. Publishing more than 20 episodes will, using simple and probably too simple logic, put you in the top 1%. Your competition isn't all podcasts in the world. But the few podcasts in your niche who didn't quit.

To many, the benefit just seems too far away. It's a pity because 30% find new podcasts to listen to using search[23] so it's a great way to get in front of completely new audiences. And did you know that 38% of listeners report purchasing things that are mentioned in podcasts?[24]

Discoverable content is distinct from other content by being searchable. This means that people will still find the content years from now. Since you produce more and more over the years, the amount of new people you will reach is accumulating over the years. That is not the case with regular social media posts. It either reaches people or it doesn't. Once it's no longer new to the algorithm, and once people are no longer commenting on it, it simply drowns in other newer content and very few people will ever again come across it.

So here is how I want you to think about creating long-term, discoverable content:

- Discoverable content creation can be **batched** and most of the tasks in the process can be outsourced to someone else. You can record 12 episodes or videos during one week and release it week by week.

- You also don't need to release every week if you don't want to. You can create a super solid limited **series** that covers questions your favourite customer has.

- Solid pieces of content can easily be **repurposed**. Let's say you create 10 videos only. That can easily be turned into 200 pieces of content - by someone who isn't you! You can manage that.

- Be strategic about your discoverable content. You can have someone create an SEO strategy for you, or analyse to find YouTube **keywords** that are not too competitive. Then create content to cover that.

- Even if your main goal is to build a YouTube channel, gain LinkedIn followers or start a podcast, always **embed** significant, SEO-based content on your website. Search engines love fresh content, and prioritise video and audio content - because that's what most people prefer to consume. Transcribe or provide a summary for those who prefer text-based content.

Now…

There is one piece of content that deserves special attention; the **book webbie-trailer**.

The what?!?

The book webbie-trailer. You know film trailers? That, but for a book, only longer like a webinar. Not one of those annoying webinars where someone keeps telling you the value is much higher but "today only, YOU can get it for less than yesterday's hamburger at MacD", or "this offer will never be available again" even though it's obviously a pre-recorded webinar and you came straight to it from an ad. No, it's not one of those at all.

The book webbie-trailer is a cleverly designed but highly **valuable** piece of long-form content. Valuable to you obvi-

"*The* book webbie-trailer *educates and inspires people to pursue the transformation they want.*

ously, but primarily to the viewers. And like always, it is designed to attract your <u>perfect</u> customers.

It presents some of the key messages and a part of the solution, without giving away everything. It **educates and inspires** people to pursue the transformation they want, solve the problem that's bothering them, and make the dream a reality.

It's the book in video format, but **entertaining** and leaving out enough for people to still be needing the book.

You can learn how to build this content on the Publishing Rebel blog where I break down the brilliant book webbie-trailer of Michael Port and Andrew Davis and provide a template to build your storyline for the video.

Get the breakdown of a book webbie-trailer.

You got that right - I invented that word
but I promise it's a real thing.

When to advertise and when not to

I get the heebie-jeebies when people claim there is only one way of marketing a book. Especially those who claim there is only one platform or one type of advertising that will work for you. First of all, you might be one of those people who don't care about how many books you sell - you are just after the authority that comes with the fact that you published a book, no matter how many you sold. People respect the effort and that you were able to get that done. If you are planning to primarily sell your books B2B, advertising seems less relevant.

Or perhaps you have raving fans and a significant audience. Subscribers to your email list, followers on social or a large and engaged community. If your organic marketing has worked well for you, you might think you'd be better off keeping pursuing those same strategies. I'd say you are missing out though. While it's fabulous that organic works for you, you have the strongest cards on your hand to achieve a great ROI on your ad campaigns.

You could:

1. Apply an event-based strategy with masterclasses during the months of the pre-launch. The events should be free but require email signup.
2. And/or go live on social and get as many as you can to grab your fantastic freebies (on a topic related to your book).

The purpose of both is to get as many of your followers onto your email list. That's a good idea even if you are not planning to run ads. Says the lady who was hacked and lost all social following on both Facebook and Instagram last year. That sh*t is not fun!

3. Filter your list and export only the most engaged people to a CSV file, ie. buyers or those with the highest opening rates. Export the entire list too.

4. Upload the lists to wherever you are planning to run ads. You should consider two campaigns:

    - A campaign to have everyone on your list consider pre-ordering your book (that's why I suggested you export the entire list too)

    - A lookalike campaign to reach new people with profiles and behaviour similar to the most engaged part of your current audience

Your ad copy should not be the same for the two campaigns since the viewers' knowledge about who you are, and how much they already trust you, is different. You can send them to either your own webpage (if you wanna send out books yourself) or to a bookstore, depending on your goals and what your book funnel looks like.

Perhaps you're among those who plan to sell most of your books on Amazon and other online bookstores. If you already have an OK-sized audience, you should engage those people in getting ranked from day one but also keep sending traffic to the book details page every day over a longer period of time to keep that ranking. Don't send out an email to 10,000 people to go buy your book and then do nothing after. Combine the above-mentioned ad strategy with an email strategy.

If you don't already have an audience but are looking to build one using your book to do so, you should consider ads. Many book coaches recommend you run Facebook ads before running Amazon ads because targeting options are plentiful. I've seen many strategies work and many that didn't.

It all depends on your goals, your current audience size and level of engagement, competition in your book category, and so many other factors. There is no one size fits all. What I encourage is that you have a plan that aligns with your goals and that you acknowledge you need to invest either time or money. One is not better than the other.

What is better though is to have a well-thought-through book funnel with some kind of upsell from your book that can finance ad campaigns. Once you have such a marketing wheel working for you, it really makes no sense not to spend more on ads since every dollar or pound will yield a higher return. Think in customer journeys and the lifetime value of a customer:

- What is the average value of a customer? How much do they spend on your products, services, or membership over, let's say 12 months? (total revenue/ number of customers)

- As long as your cost to acquire a customer, on average, is lower than the CLV (Customer Lifetime Value), you should keep running ads and working on optimising your book funnel.

The only difference in advertising books over other products or services is that you have book-specific advertising platforms available, like Goodreads, BookBub, Amazon, etc. The way it works isn't all that different.

To summarise:

- Run ads if you can get a positive ROI (lifetime value greater than the cost of acquisition)
- Show ads where your audience is
- Qualify your targeting using your own data when possible
- Use different copy for different levels of knowledge that the person seeing the ad has about you

Getting in front of crowds

Whether your dream is to become a sought-after and well-paid keynote speaker, to be able to connect and interact with audiences directly, or are driven by the opportunities to travel and expand your network with other speakers and/or colleagues in your field, you need a book to boost your public speaking career. You already know that. It's even likely that's the very reason you are reading this book.

This book does not have a goal to advise on how to become a public speaker. Instead, I want to inspire how you can use public speaking to promote your book or use your book to promote yourself as a public speaker.

The value of a copy of your book is higher than your print cost. This means you have the option to present your fee in different ways. Consider reducing your fee if they buy copies of your book for the participants. Or you could simply add your print cost to your fee and include books as a "bonus". Again, you should know the average lifetime value of a customer and ask questions about who is in the audience before making your offer. Even a lower fee may be highly profitable if people in the audience are likely to sign up for your membership or buy your digital course.

Not all event managers will allow you to promote your book directly, so you need to think beyond simply adding it to your slide deck.

Here are some uncommon and out-of-the-box strategies you can consider:

- **Seed Curiosity:** Throughout your presentation, drop hints, anecdotes, or references that are related to the content of your book. Make these references intriguing and thought-provoking, sparking curiosity among the audience about the source of these insights.

- **Offer Additional Resources:** Towards the end of your presentation, provide the audience with a list of additional resources that can further explore the topic you discussed. Include a mention of your book alongside other relevant books, articles, websites, or podcasts. This positions your book as a valuable resource without explicitly promoting it.

- **Q&A Strategy:** During the Q&A session, respond to questions by incorporating insights or examples from your book, without explicitly mentioning it. By providing valuable and in-depth answers, you pique the audience's interest and prompt them to seek out more information - hopefully leading them to your book.

- **Post-Presentation Handouts:** Prepare handouts or one-pagers summarising the main points of your presentation. Include a list of recommended readings or resources at the end, with your book included among them. This allows the audience to take something tangible with them and discover your book at their own pace.

- **Speaker bio:** Ask the person who introduces you to mention that you are an author of book X, or include it on the very last slide in your deck along with your contact information. If that's not possible, invite the audience to connect with you on LinkedIn and have a banner that shows the book and where to get it.

- **Strategic Networking:** Spend time with the audience after finishing your talk. Stay beside the stage or in the hallway if it's a bigger venue with someone else speaking after you. Build relationships based on shared interests, and let the conversation naturally lead to your book. Your new business card may be a pixi-version of your book or have an image of the book on it along with a QR code to learn more.

- **Case Studies:** Casually mention a case study from your book or research you made when writing your book without much mention of your book at all. Make it subtle. People are already wondering if you have a book and will find it if it's for them. By establishing yourself as an authority and providing valuable insights, you create a natural curiosity that drives people to seek out your published work.

You can also creatively define what a stage is. The point is that you get in front of a bigger crowd (not necessarily on a traditional stage), capture the attention of the right people, and have great stories to share long after the event.

You can find funky ideas for event-based marketing in the Fandango section of this book.

In general, think about how you can inspire people to buy more than one book. Create compelling offers creatively that you can offer not only related to your public speaking activities and own events, but also reaching out to corporations and companies, and industry associations. Is your book something employees would appreciate as a Christmas present? Could event hosts be interested in adding them to swag bags, even if you are not a speaker at the event? Could you add different bonuses for different amounts of books purchased?

I don't need to mention, it's essential to align your strategies with your target audience. As a final remark, consider if you would benefit the most from direct sales (usually at a discounted price), or from a contribution to a great ranking online. Having even one B2B company ordering your book online during launch week or shortly thereafter thereby helping the book rank and reach a lot more people, might be worth considering. Always consider when to sacrifice short-term profit for long-term success.

Getting reviews

Many authors love reviews but for the wrong reasons. Or at least not for all of the great reasons. What I notice is that authors tend to be concerned about the judgement: Good or bad? - which often translates into: Am I good enough? Who will see if I get bad reviews? I will die if someone I know sees it.

Reviews usually matter. Social proof accounts for ⅔ of purchasing activity. This is what we do - we look to peers for advice rather than listen to what marketers want us to think. And as previously mentioned briefly, reviews are important signals for the algorithms to learn who is likely to like (buy) your book.

Not all audiences care much about social proof - unless it's a really cool person they know who recommends it. And you might not care much either if you plan to mostly sell books in bulk to companies or at events where people already had the chance to listen to you and already see you as an expert. They won't care much what other people think. Also, a book is rather inexpensive. Lots of people won't bother to read any reviews at all.

But the algorithm cares.

- Not only did the reader consider your book (he or she read the book details page)
- Not only did the reader choose the book (purchased)
- He or she came back to tell others about the book (posted a review)

Add to the mix all the data kept on file about that person's usual buying behaviour - and how many Amazon visitors (or any other popular store) have a similar pattern. They'd be idiots not to put emphasis on reviews.

So in short: If you care about online sales, you should care about reviews.

So how do you get readers to review your book? Well, first of all, pay attention to store guidelines. Inviting your entire family to review (using the same surname) or inviting everyone to a big party and having everyone review (using the same IP address at the venue) - or outright paying for reviews - won't work. The store will detect the pattern and simply delete them. And you really should care that the people reviewing are people in your target audience. If you are using reviews as a tool to enhance sales, make sure the algorithm will look for more of your people.

Getting reviews can be hard work unless you have engaged fans already. Find ways to have people ready to give reviews as early as possible. Warm up your audience and make them desire to help you in your launch. This means you are being generous first and then making your ask. Find ways to collect a list of people willing to help, a book launch team.

I am not gonna go into details on how to build and engage a book launch team here. But the basics include:

- Give them a PDF with a watermark 1-2 weeks before launch, asking them not to share. Tell them they received it as a trusted person. Reach out personally to as many as possible (you'll likely experience you'll even make sales during those conversations so it may be well worth it). Show your interest in them.

- The moment your book is on Amazon, send the PDF again and ask for review. Tell them it would be even better if they purchase the ebook - or download it from the store if you are running a "free" campaign. Explain how this helps you.

- Create a system like an Excel spreadsheet to follow up. You should reach out personally but you can have someone monitor and update the information as reviews come in. Don't send more than 2 emails and 1-2 personal messages, depending on your relationship.

- Ask them to send their review to you so you can thank them properly. Then when they do, ask if you may use it in testimonials on your website. Make sure you stop any automated email sequence asking them to do something they already did for you.

Consider asking for reviews for the audio version.

- First of all, people will be able to listen to them directly from your website without you having to share any files. You can upload it on a course platform as an audio product or podcast and only give access to invited people.

- Secondly, when you publish your audiobook exclusively through Amazon-owned ACX, you get up to 100 promo codes per audiobook. Other platforms also offer promo codes. These codes are a great way to gift copies of the audiobook. In turn, your readers – or in this case, listeners – will hopefully leave a review.

Apart from your own network and current audience, you can find book lovers and book bloggers who are passionate about giving reviews. Here are some ideas to search for people to give reviews:

- Google: [title of competing book] +book blogger or [title of competing book] +book reviews
- #bookstagram on Instagram or #booktok on Tik-Tok to find bloggers who your book will fit (they won't accept you if it's not a good fit so spend your time wisely)
- YouTube: search for #booktuber (channels that share videos about books they're reading) or #booktuber nonfiction or #booktuber +topic or +competing title
- Twitter: search for @BookTuber
- Reedsy has a list of book bloggers:
- https://blog.reedsy.com/book-review-blogs/
- BookBloggerList.com - choose nonfiction and the subcategory that fits your book
- Other authors (we are back to why you need to plan your network expansion ahead of time)

the FANDANGO

This section of the book offers funky, weird, out-of-the-box, unconventional and fun marketing ideas.

- **Flash Mob Book Reading**

  Organise a flash mob in a public space where participants suddenly gather and start reading excerpts from your book aloud. This unique and attention-grabbing event will create buzz and intrigue among onlookers.

- **Collaborate with Comedians**

  Team up with a comedian or comedy group to create a humorous performance centred around the themes in your book. The comedic twist will make your message more memorable and help you reach new audiences who enjoy comedy shows.

- **Storytelling Events**

  Organise unique storytelling events where attendees can share their personal stories related to the topic of your book. Encourage participants to relate their experiences to the themes discussed in your book, and offer signed copies as rewards for the most captivating stories. The events can be part of a national tour, or a virtual.

- **Host fringe events inspired by your book**

  Design an interactive workshop that combines elements from your book with practical exercises and activities. Offer this workshop as fringe events at conferences, corporate events, or even specialised retreats to provide attendees with a unique learning experience.

- **Host a Book Trailer Premiere**

  Create an enticing and visually captivating book trailer video that captures the essence of your non-fiction book. Organise a premiere event where you showcase the trailer on a big screen, accompanied by live music, performances, or guest speakers. Make it an immersive experience that generates excitement and curiosity about your book. The crazier the theme, the better. Make the whole thing Insta-worthy or a TikTok no-brainer.

- **Host a virtual summit**

  Collab with peers with similar audiences (size and pain/desire) to organise a full-day virtual event and take turns in presenting high-value content to the participants. If you are all authors, you can consider a special price for a limited-time book offer.

- **Make endorsing your book an experience**

  Dan Gingiss has a light bulb on the cover of his book 'The Experience Maker'. When he sent out 100 copies ahead of his book launch to have influential people endorse it, he built a real lightbulb into the book. This had people create and share videos, recommending people buy the book.

- **Industry event targeting**

  Shortly after I launched my first book 'Marketing Made Human', I participated in Social Media Marketing World. During those days, I ran ads targeting fans of Social Media Examiner (the event organiser) who were currently in San Diego. The 5,000 participants saw my ads every time they opened an app to post about the event. This strategy kicked the book to #1 on Amazon.

- **Virtual Reality (VR) Experiences**

  Develop virtual reality experiences that allow readers to step into the world of your book. Have them meet the people showcased in your book. Let them join a panel discussion. Have a virtual cocktail with other fans.

- **Podcast Drama Series**

  Instead of traditional podcast interviews or discussions, produce a fictionalised audio drama series inspired by the stories or topics covered in your book. Engage talented voice actors, sound designers, and writers to create an immersive audio experience that keeps listeners hooked and eager to learn more.

- **Satellite Book Launches**

  Host book launch events in unconventional locations such as rooftops, boats, or other unique venues. Consider partnering with local businesses or organisations to create memorable settings that align with your book's themes and generate excitement among attendees.

- **Scavenger hunt**

  Put clues into your book for readers to find. Design it so they need to make a reasonable effort to put together a sentence, a code or something else that will give exclusive access to something they desire.

- **Make up a national holiday**

  Invent a "Serendipitous Story Swap day", "Funky Fitness Flashmob Festival", "Biodiversity Bonanza Bash", or "Plastic Pledge Parade". Something related to your business. Create a video with (fake) history of the holiday and rituals (what people need to do). Think of what might make people want to create and share content. Add a national day hashtag.

Please take 2 minutes to do this

We have come to the end of this book. As you know, getting reviews is hard work and it would be a great help if you would write a quick one for this book on Amazon.

Can you help me with that?

Just go to Amazon.com and search using some of the words that describe what you learned in this book:

Nonfiction author

I want to become an author

How to become a nonfiction author

How to selfpublish a book

Writing a book guide

How to create a book

Tips writing a book

If nothing else works, search by title and author.

Author Bio

Malene Bendtsen is an author of 3 nonfiction books and a business strategist teaching experts, teachers, public speakers and other freedom seekers how to write, publish and market their nonfiction books.

She is also the former CEO of a self publishing company covering Latin America and the editor of dozens of nonfiction books, which on average, sold 5x market average and created significant business growth for the authors.

Malene is determined to find new ways for authors to connect with their audience and strategically use their books to build their businesses. As a publishing rebel and a knowledge liberator, there are no darlings she won't kill.

Connect:
mb@malenebendtsen.com
LinkedIn.com/in/bendtsen
@publishingrebel (Insta, the Tok, and the Tube)
Publishing-rebel.com

Other books by Malene Bendtsen

Author Coaching

You might be wondering how I can help you take the next step NOW:

- Done-with-you and done-for-you services
- One-to-one author coaching
- Access to author platform and group coaching

Will you love it? Yes, if you loved this book, you will.

"Every author needs a village. You have been an incredible book coach. I could not have done this without you"
- Dr. Poornima Luthra

"Massive thanks for giving me not only the proverbial kick up but also for giving me a structure to get the squillions of ideas out of my head and on paper!"
- Sarah Clay

"I am in love with my book and the process"
- Gitte Madelaire

Don't let the dream slip away from you again.

There will never be enough time and you will need to give the book priority for it to happen.

Vamos!

www.publishing-rebel.com

Endnotes

1   https://www.create.ac.uk/wp-content/uploads/2022/12/Authors-earnings-report-DEF.pdf
2   Authors Licensing & Collecting Society
3   Writers' Union of Canada
4   Authors Guild
5   National Survey of Australian Book Authors
6   https://www.statista.com/statistics/473144/half-year-book-sales-revenue-format-usa/
7   https://www.statista.com/statistics/473144/half-year-book-sales-revenue-format-usa
8   https://www.statista.com/statistics/284362/book-sales-revenue-in-the-united-kingdom-uk
9   https://www.statista.com/statistics/305733/consumer-audio-book-download-sales-revenue-in-the-uk
10 https://www.statista.com/statistics/1265481/ebook-print-book-cagr-revenue-worldwide/
11 https://www.statista.com/statistics/859435/hardback-book-sales-revenue/
12 https://wordsrated.com/global-book-sales-statistics/
13 https://wordsrated.com/nonfiction-book-sales-statistics/
14 https://blog.submittable.com/publishing-industry-trends/
15 https://goodereader.com/blog/e-book-news/indie-authors-triumphing-over-sexism-in-the-publishing-industry
16 https://scribemedia.com/book-sales/
17 https://scribemedia.com/book-royalties/
18 https://www.entrepreneur.com/growing-a-business/5-marketing-tips-to-take-from-beyonce/429782
19 https://www.tonerbuzz.com/blog/paper-books-vs-ebooks-statistics/
20 https://wordsrated.com/audiobook-statistics/
21 https://wordsrated.com/amazon-publishing-statistics/
22 https://selfpublishingadvice.org/facts-and-figures-about-self-publishing-the-impact-and-influence-of-indie-authors/
23 https://www.buzzsprout.com/blog/podcast-statistics
24 https://nealschaffer.com/podcast-statistics/